Wellington Architecture

Wellington Architecture

A Walking Guide

John Walsh

Photography by Patrick Reynolds

MASSEY UNIVERSITY PRESS

In memory of Gerald Melling,
1943–2012

CONTENTS

INTRODUCTION

I was born in Wellington and grew up there, and the town, as compact and confined as a medieval city-state, intensely impressed itself on me, in the most impressionable part of my life. My mother had moved to Wellington, where she met my father, and they were married in the church at St Gerard's Monastery. I remember the Freyberg Pool, where I learned to swim; the summer lights strung on the Norfolk pines along Oriental Parade; and the council yard where my father worked, next to the Herd Street Post and Telegraph Building. My high school was near the old National Art Gallery and Dominion Museum; we'd be sent to Mass at St Mary of the Angels and, in blazers and ties, despatched from Wellington Railway Station on rugby expeditions into the hinterlands of the Hutt Valley.

My first part-time job was at James Smith's Department Store; I'd visit the Central Library, the old one, with its banks of index card catalogues, and Parson's Bookshop in Massey House, and the hippy stores in the shabby Edwardian buildings on Cuba Street. The first concerts I went to were in the Town Hall; I remember a Dadaist performance in the Hannah Playhouse. When I climbed up the steps on my way to university I'd pass Jellicoe Towers, designed by the father of a fellow student and friend. One of my sisters worked in the Departmental Building on Stout Street; my brother rowed at the Star Boating Club.

These buildings don't just have a remembered existence, I'm happy to say. They're still there, even if they're not all serving their original purpose. And, I'm also happy to say, they're in this book, a guide to the significant buildings constructed in central Wellington since the 1860s, and to the architects who designed them. The book is an overview of the architecture of the city and, I hope, an introduction to the city through its architecture. It's a walking guide to a very walkable city — the city as seen from its footpaths, although many of the buildings on the five itineraries, none much longer than 3 kilometres, are open to public visitation or use. In the main, the buildings are urban-scaled. They were designed for banks, businesses and government departments. They're churches, clubs, courts, libraries, museums, hotels, apartments, and just a few are private houses. These are buildings that were designed with a public face to take their place in the city's streetscape.

Wellington's natural environment has given the city's architects a hard act to follow and challenging conditions to address. Its landforms are dramatic; its climate is, shall we say, bracing; its seismic circumstances are precarious; its harbour is wonderful but often windswept. It is a city of tempers and moods, sometimes foul, but often fair. Te Ahumairangi (Tinakori) Hill broods over the government end of town while Oriental Bay on a fine, calm day looks like a Mediterranean transposition. For a few blocks around Featherston Street, Wellington has the dense solidity of a Midwestern American downtown, while the Botanic Garden is a time-trip to the Edwardian era. The most harmonious interventions in the local topography are the public paths and steps, with their white wooden rails offering the puffing pedestrian safety and support, that ascend the hills on both sides of the harbour.

The human history of the place now known as Wellington goes back more than a thousand years to the arrival of the Polynesian navigator Kupe. Occupation probably dates from the twelfth or thirteenth centuries. The original name for Wellington was Te Whanganui-a-Tara (the great harbour of Tara), a title that recognises a son of the explorer Whātonga, a captain of the waka *Kurahaupō*, which landed on the Māhia Peninsula in Hawke's Bay. In the early nineteenth century, Ngāti Ira from Hawke's Bay was probably the dominant tribe at Te Whanganui-a-Tara, but the iwi was driven out by incursions from around 1820 by tribes from the north, especially from the Taranaki region. At the time of the signing of Te Tiriti o Waitangi in 1840 — the year after the arrival at Te Whanganui-a-Tara of the first European settlers in a ship sent by the colonising New Zealand Company — the inhabitants of the area were mainly Te Ātiawa, Taranaki, Ngāti Ruanui, Ngāti Tama and Ngāti Toa. At this time, there were well-established pā near the harbour at Pipitea and Te Aro, and the first settler encampments coalesced around these sites.

With a tug of their forelocks, and profound indifference to indigenous opinion, the settlers followed the direction of the New Zealand Company and petitioned the most famous British imperial figure for permission to borrow his name for their town. Hence, Wellington. The first European buildings in the new settlement were rudimentary, and the architecture, to use a flattering term, of Wellington remained simple for decades. Two questions that have always been relevant and interconnected throughout the city's history immediately presented themselves: Where to build? And how to build?

The settlers' preferred town site at the comparatively sheltered south end of the harbour did not offer a lot of flat land. Reclamation was the answer to this problem, and Wellington has nibbled away at its harbour for 170 years since. The solution brought its own dilemmas because reclaimed land, less stable in any circumstance, is especially insecure in a city built upon a major earthquake fault. Consequently, the story of architecture in Wellington is also a seismic engineering story — a chronicle of caissons and concrete piles, steel reinforcing, base-isolation and retrofitting. The Modernist censure of building ornamentation was to an extent redundant in Wellington; architects soon learned that, on the city's buildings, anything decoratively attached — statues, balustrades, turrets, clock towers — was likely to be shaken loose.

Wellington's colonists were familiar with buildings made of stone and brick but in their new settlement issues of confidence and supply made masonry construction problematic. Earthquakes, such as the very large 1855 quake, left their mark on the civic consciousness, even if Wellingtonians have long been adept at repressing their memories of seismic incidents. Not only did inadequately reinforced masonry buildings present mortal danger, but the Wellington region lacked stone suitable for construction. (Stone from other parts of New Zealand, and from abroad, was imported for sparing use on significant buildings.) Bricks were made in the city — the best by prisoners at Mount Cook Gaol — but they could not safely support structures more than a couple of storeys high.

For the first two generations of settlement, then, Wellington was predominantly a timber town. Wood was relatively cheap and easy to work, and a feature of Wellington's Victorian-era architecture was the timber expression of stone detailing. (The classic example of this design trait is the 1876 Government

Building.) But timber, too, had an obvious drawback in a city lit by oil lamps and candles and heated by open fires. Buildings burned down so frequently that in 1877 the generally laissez-faire city council mandated the cladding of new central-city buildings in 'incombustible' materials. For the next 40 years many buildings not captured by this ordinance — churches, often, but also, in 1907, Parliament House — went up in smoke.

Before, and even after, the advent of reinforced concrete construction around the turn of the twentieth century, Wellington's inhabitants showed remarkable resilience in the face of the existential threats to the city's fabric (and their persons). Buildings destroyed by fire were replaced with amazing alacrity. For the Victorians and Edwardians, 'build back better' was not a slogan but an expectation. Architecture, whether in replacement or novel form, was a barometer of colonial ambition. Its occurrence was a testament to the resolve of building owners and users, but also to the simplicity of building materials and technologies, the sufficiency of craft knowledge and skills, and the straightforwardness of what we now call the consenting process.

As the city grew it spread its footprint, following the roads and tramlines that extended around the harbour and into Te Aro. Before the First World War, the identity, and urbanity, of Wellington was becoming shaped by the strong and particular character of its main streets: Lambton Quay, which follows the old shoreline; Willis Street, which meets it, and continues south, eventually in parallel with Cuba Street, which itself almost intersects with Courtenay Place; The Terrace, rising above the CBD, and its antipode, across the harbour, Oriental Parade. These streets are the basis for the routes in this book, with the exception of Courtenay Place, which is an interesting street without — except for under-repair St James Theatre — significant buildings. (Also, parts of Courtenay Place demand a wide berth, especially at night.)

The development of the city can be traced in the evolution of its architecture. Because Wellington is the capital city it has important buildings, constructed for the government and for companies that wanted to be proximate to it. For much of the twentieth century these buildings were commissioned by the organisations, public and private, that owned and occupied them. This made a qualitative difference. The government set an example through the work of its own design office, configured initially as the office of the Colonial Architect and then as the office of the Government Architect. Architects in the office, sometimes to the annoyance of private practitioners, designed a wide range of central Wellington buildings — apartments, post and telegraph offices, a police station, library, observatory, dental school, and Parliament House.

One result of the economic deregulation and bureaucratic restructuring that began in the 1980s — and saw the demise of the Government Architect's office — is that government departments have become building tenants, not owners. Corporations, too, now take out space in developers' buildings. Between the wars, the old regime produced the high-quality corporate head offices clustered in the neighbourhood of Featherston Street and Customhouse Quay, and in the 1960s and 1970s, the client-ownership model yielded well-built Brutalist towers near Parliament. Perhaps it's a coincidence, but since 2000, several large Wellington buildings constructed by developers and tenanted by government departments or corporations have failed within a decade of their opening.

Whether of private or public provenance, Wellington's buildings, from the start of colonial settlement to the First World War, were revivalist iterations of the Gothic, Classical and Baroque styles. (Such was the case in all contemporary colonial cities.) Between the wars, Art Deco, Moderne and Stripped Classical were the dominant styles. Modernism, in its International Style and Brutalist forms, came relatively late to Wellington but it also stayed relatively late. Modernist buildings were still being completed in the middle of the 1980s, even as Post-modernism was entering its second decade in the city. Of all the city's architecture, only the early Gothic Revival buildings, such as Old St Paul's, and Modernist buildings such as Massey House, Clifton Towers and the Meteorological Office, could be meaningfully connected to a movement. Others, such as St Mary of the Angels, were certainly located in a tradition. For many more buildings, though, design was less a matter of conviction than of mastering the various dialects of a pattern language.

Some eras in Wellington's architecture have been stronger than others, and in a couple of periods the city led the nation. As mentioned, the inter-war years produced a crop of impressive institutional and commercial buildings, and also small apartment buildings. During the Depression, being the seat of government and the site of corporate head offices was beneficial to Wellington, as was the Keynesian orientation of the Labour Party that came to power in the mid-1930s. The other period of Wellington's architectural eminence was the decade from the mid-1960s, when Ian Athfield and Roger Walker sprang a series of Post-modernist surprises. Their architecture was a jolt to a staid city.

That's the architectural story. What of Wellington's architects? In general, and over time, several distinguishing characteristics are discernible. One, very noticeably, is gender. Up until the last few decades of the twentieth century, almost all architects were male. In this, architecture, in Wellington and across New Zealand, was similar to professions such as law and medicine. However, specific factors reinforced architecture's same-sex caste. In the nineteenth and early twentieth centuries, the practice of architecture and the organisation of architecture offices was not so different from the guild system of the medieval building trades. Many architects in colonial Wellington were builders who had picked up sufficient design experience to unilaterally rebrand themselves. Another main route into architecture was via apprenticeship or pupillage, a process in which young men paid to be 'articled' to established architects or firms. Even when architecture became more professional, as tertiary education became an entry-level qualification — the University of Auckland started teaching architecture in 1926 but Victoria University of Wellington's School of Architecture didn't open until 1975 — the hierarchical structure of architecture firms echoed that of the ancient gendered guilds.

The architects, or the men who called themselves architects, in nineteenth-century Wellington were mainly immigrants from England and Scotland. That changed in the early twentieth century as Wellington architecture became more of a home-grown, even parochial pursuit. Several Australian architects, notably Llewellyn Edwin Williams, practised in the city, and clients occasionally called on the big-building expertise of Melbourne and Sydney firms. In the late 1930s, some very able European émigré architects, such as Frederick Newman and Ernst Plischke, worked in Wellington, usually for the Government Architect's office.

For two decades from the mid-1950s, an expanding Ministry of Works imported architects from Britain. In the history of twentieth-century Wellington — and New Zealand — architectural practice, Māori hardly got a look-in; John Scott, architect of Futuna Chapel, was, for a few years, a rare Māori presence on the local architecture scene. Even the interventions of practices from other cities in New Zealand have been limited, although some have been notable: Auckland-based Gummer & Ford designed the National Art Gallery and Dominion Museum, the old Central Library and the State Insurance Building, and Jasmax designed Te Papa; Cecil Wood from Christchurch designed the new St Paul's Cathedral.

In their professional and personal lives, Wellington architects, for a century and a half, tended to have the unexceptional habits and interests of their class. Architects, especially in the decades before the Second World War, were clubbable, out of both social inclination and professional self-interest. (Networking brought clients.) They lawn-bowled — until golf became more popular — and they belonged to gentlemen's clubs; they enjoyed motoring — the attraction of architects to stylish cars is perennial — and gardening was a common passion. Yacht-ownership was a sign of professional success. Many architects were Masons, perhaps unsurprisingly, given Freemasonry's link to the old stonemason guilds. Some served as city councillors, especially in the decades before the First World War; one, Michael Fowler, served as mayor (1974–1983). Military service was another shared experience of the city's architects in the first half of the twentieth century. Many careers were interrupted, affected or even definitively ended by war.

Before the Second World War, architects' attention tended to be confined to the individual building. Edmund Anscombe, who was very active in the 1930s, was exceptional in his concern for exhibiting architecture and proposing affordable multi-unit housing. The architectural focus widened from the building to the city in the 1950s and 1960s. Younger Modernist architects, returned from studying in America and Britain and visiting buildings by Le Corbusier and Mies van der Rohe, found an outlet for urban advocacy in the Wellington Architectural Centre. Two decades later, Ian Athfield stressed the importance of the spaces between buildings, not just the buildings themselves.

The practice of architecture now is complex, far more so than it was in the nineteenth century, and significantly more so than it was in the twentieth century. Projects require more collaboration and this is fostering, in architecture firms, greater inclusivity. For example, in terms of gender diversity, three of the prominent Wellington practices whose work features in this book — Athfield Architects, Studio Pacific Architecture and Warren and Mahoney — have female principals: Rachel Griffiths and Sophie Vial, Lianne Cox, and Katherine Skipper. On larger projects, it is not really possible — or considered appropriate — to attribute a building's design to a single hand. Ath was the last 'starchitect' in the Wellington design firmament.

This wasn't how things were arranged for most of the period covered in this book. Until the start of this century, design direction was ascribed to, and claimed by, the man with his name on the practice shingle. It is therefore possible to periodise — if not define — Wellington's architecture by reference to a series of outstanding architects who designed buildings that can still be seen from the city's footpaths: Thomas Turnbull, that eminent Victorian; Frederick de Jersey Clere, busy for more than 40 years on either side of the turn of the twentieth century; William Gray Young, at his height between the wars, when Edmund Anscombe and William Henry Gummer were also practising in the city; Ian Athfield, from the 1960s through to the end of the twentieth century.

And this is not to slight the work of other architects who have contributed to Wellington's architectural legacy, architects such as Frederick Thatcher, Llewellyn Edwin Williams, Government Architects John Campbell and John Thomas Mair, Cyril Hawthorn Mitchell, Ernst Plischke, James Beard, Bill Alington, Gordon Moller and Roger Walker. The list of good buildings in Te Whanganui-a-Tara is long, and no doubt will get longer, as the pool of people designing them becomes wider and deeper.

A NOTE ABOUT ACCESS AND CLASSIFICATIONS

This book is a walking guide to central Wellington — the city from its footpaths — but many of the buildings are open for visits or use.

ROUTE 1: HARBOURSIDE
The commercial building at 10 Waterloo Quay has a café, and the former Wellington Harbour Board Office and Bond Store is now Wellington Museum. Te Wharewaka o Pōneke has a café and runs waka tours, and the Wellington Free Ambulance Building houses a bar. Te Papa, New Zealand's national museum, is open every day except Christmas Day.

ROUTE 2: TE ARO FLAT
The Embassy is a working cinema, and the building has a streetside café. Moore Wilson's is a large and popular food store. Wesley Methodist Church is open for Sunday services. The former National Bank Te Aro building is an upmarket restaurant, and the buildings at 101–127 Cuba Street house several bars and restaurants. The Michael Fowler Centre is an event venue. The New Zealand Racing Conference Building has housed a ground-floor café for 30 years, and the Wellington City Gallery (formerly the Central Library) also has a long-running café, Nikau.

ROUTE 3: CENTRAL SPINE
The Hall of Memories is a publicly accessible building but at the time of writing is closed for earthquake-strengthening. On Willis Street, the First Church of Christ, Scientist is often open, even apart from Sunday services, as are St Peter's and St John's churches. St Mary of the Angels is open daily. Plimmer House is an upmarket restaurant. There are cafés in the Majestic Centre, Telecom (Spark) Central and at the street level of the tower at 1 Willis Street.

ROUTE 4: CBD

The Supreme Court and Old High Court (former Supreme Court) may be visited on guided tours. The former DIC Department Store building has several retail outlets, and the old Bank of New Zealand Buildings (Nos 1, 2 and 3) are now conjoined as a retail arcade. 20 Customhouse Quay has a ground-floor café, and the former Wellesley Club has a café and bar. Wellington Railway Station still functions, in large part, as a railway station.

ROUTE 5: WEST SIDE

The Carter Observatory is now a museum or 'visitor attraction', open daily. The Hunter Building is on the Kelburn campus of Victoria University of Wellington, which has a small and interesting art gallery — Adam Art Gallery Te Pātaka Toi — which is open to the public, and several cafés. St Andrew's on The Terrace is open daily. Guided tours of the buildings in the parliamentary complex, including the 'Beehive', Parliament House and General Assembly Library, are on offer to the public. The Cathedral of St Paul is open daily. The National Library of New Zealand, and its well-patronised café and well-curated exhibition gallery, is open on weekdays and Saturday mornings. Old St Paul's Church is open most days, and tours may be booked. Futuna Chapel stages open days several times a year, and also special events.

As noted in the text, many of the buildings in this guide have been designated as an 'Historic Place' by the government's heritage agency, Heritage New Zealand Pouhere Taonga. This appellation comes in two grades: Category 1, which signifies a place of special or outstanding historical or cultural interest, and Category 2, which indicates historical or cultural interest (but not so special). A collective heritage appellation, 'Historic Area', has been applied to the 'Seven Sisters' row of houses on Oriental Parade. It should be noted that a heritage listing of any type does not guarantee protection. Also, heritage listing is skewed towards buildings constructed before the Second World War, although Modern-era buildings, such as Futuna Chapel, are starting to make it onto the heritage list.

ROUTE 1:
HARBOURSIDE

CIRCA 3 KILOMETRES

Te Whanganui-a-Tara, or Wellington Harbour, as it has been more lately called, is the great natural and economic asset of the city founded on its shore. A walk around the harbour is a tour of a century and a half of Wellington's built history, including the architecture of the old working port and of Oriental Parade, New Zealand's best waterfront promenade. The route starts with buildings the Harbour Board constructed on reclaimed land in the years of its Victorian and Edwardian pomp and finishes near the far end of Oriental Parade, with some of the inter-war apartment buildings that announced the advent of Wellington's urbanity. The route — which of course can be walked in either direction, but the afternoon is much more benign on west-facing Oriental Parade — includes New Zealand's national museum, buildings for boats and waka, Modernist flats and two city landmarks, St Gerard's Monastery and Freyberg Pool.

Wellington Harbour Board Shed 21

28 Waterloo Quay

James Marchbanks, Wellington Harbour Board Engineer, 1910
Historic Place Category 1

On the night of 9 March 1909, Wellingtonians were treated to what local newspaper *The Dominion* described as 'a magnificent scene' on the city's wharves as an early 1880s timber warehouse containing hundreds of bales of flax went up in flames. Big fires in the city's timber buildings were not uncommon, and accounts of conflagrations read less like reports than reviews. 'A great deal of picturesqueness was added to the scene when the rigging of the barque *Hippola* took fire,' the *Dominion* article continued, 'and the reflection of the flames against the dull waters of the harbour made a bright effect.' Another *Dominion* correspondent, 'Domenica', claiming to write about the fire from 'a woman's point of view', focused on the crowd's couture. Noting that the wharf fire attracted a larger female audience than the fire that destroyed the timber Parliament buildings in December 1907, 'Domenica' regretted that most of the watching women 'were disappointingly well dressed' after early arrivals had been 'hastily and interestingly attired'.

The odds of fire-prompted public displays of déshabillé lengthened when the ruined building was quickly replaced by a brick wool store with steel beams and concrete columns. Built right to the street edge at Waterloo Quay, the three-level building, known as Shed 21, is an imposing piece of Edwardian warehouse architecture, expressly functional but stolidly handsome with its long rows of arched windows, simple cornice and decorative parapet around its saw-tooth roof. The design was drawn up under the supervision of James Marchbanks (1862–1947), the Harbour Board's Chief Engineer from 1908 to 1932. His son Donald (1901–1987) served in the same role from 1945 to 1966. In the early 2000s, Shed 21 was converted into apartments by Athfield Architects.

10 Waterloo Quay
('Kumutoto Site 10')

Athfield Architects, 2018

Architects and engineers have complementary skills but a sometimes wary relationship. In satisfying the equally weighted Vitruvian criteria for a well-designed building, the roles, in general, are clear: firmness, or structural integrity, is ensured by the engineer; delight, or aesthetic appeal, is the province of the architect; and utility, or functional performance, is a shared responsibility. This consensus usually survives professional chauvinism, although among themselves architects might mutter that the engineer's job is to make a building stay up so it can look good, while engineers might say it doesn't matter so much what a building looks like as long as it stays up. But whatever the variance in professional perspectives, the balance of power is often dictated by circumstances.

On Wellington's wharves, engineers have called the shots from the start of William Ferguson's long reign (1884–1908) as the Harbour Board Engineer (see overleaf). Their primacy is understandable: Wellington is seismically vulnerable and its port is located on reclaimed land, 155 hectares of the harbour having been filled in since the 1850s. The challenges of building in a place where nature strongly suggests you shouldn't were demonstrated by the structural failure of two large harbourside buildings, constructed in the first decade of this century, in the 2016 magnitude 7.8 Kaikōura earthquake. These precedents were fresh when Athfield Architects collaborated with engineers Dunning Thornton on the design of a five-level office building on the site of a former wharf carpark. The building's long, glazed superstructure sits on base isolators above 1200 steel-reinforced concrete piles, a foundation that allows the building 65 centimetres of lateral movement during an earthquake. The architecture made possible by this engineering is most dramatically evident in the cantilevering that provides a portico at the building's south end, and colonnades that offer welcome pedestrian shelter along the east and west elevations.

Sheds 11 and 13

41 Customhouse Quay and 60 Lady Elizabeth Lane

William Ferguson, Wellington Harbour Board Engineer, 1905
Historic Place Category 1

In 1884, 1925 ships unloaded 106,000 tons of freight at Wellington's port and loaded 25,000 tons; in 1907, 3395 ships delivered 420,000 tons and picked up 135,000 tons. This growth coincided with and was largely enabled by the tenure as Harbour Board Engineer (and also Board Secretary and Treasurer) of William Ferguson (1852–1935). Ferguson was an engineering graduate of Trinity College, Dublin, who immigrated to New Zealand in 1883. The year after his arrival, he was appointed Wellington Harbour Board Engineer. Ferguson was very capable. Under his leadership Wellington's port was recognised as one of the most efficient in the southern hemisphere, a particular advantage being the hydraulic system Ferguson invented to power the port's cranes, winches and wool presses.

In 1904, after the latest harbour reclamation, Ferguson's staff designed two warehouses, now known as Sheds 11 and 13. The matching buildings, each 52 metres long × 10 metres wide, were constructed of load-bearing bricks on a foundation of tōtara piles held together by concrete and steel beams. Timber trusses support roofs with skylights that run almost the length of the buildings; the pitch of the skylights and the ornate lintels above the buildings' large sliding doors lend the warehouses a Dutch Colonial appearance.

Not long after the warehouses' construction, in October 1907, the local press reported 'a mad sensation in the city': the Harbour Board's Engineer and 'walking encyclopaedia' had resigned. As one newspaper remarked, with slight hyperbole, the Board for years 'had existed chiefly and almost solely for endorsing [Ferguson's] views'. So, when a couple of new Harbour Board members, one of them a former Harbour Board employee, told Ferguson not to give his opinion unless he was asked for it, the Engineer quit. (The Harbour Board later had to get him back as a consultant.) Shed 11 now houses the New Zealand Portrait Gallery, and Shed 13 a commercial tenant.

Shed 7 (Wellington Harbour Board Wharf Offices and Woolstore)

Jervois Quay, 1 Queens Wharf and 63 Customhouse Quay

Clere, Fitzgerald & Richmond, 1896
Historic Place Category 1

In the New Zealand settler tradition of laconic nomenclature — North and South Island set the deadpan precedent — one of Wellington's most ornate buildings came to be called a shed. The building, when it was completed in 1896, was named the Wellington Harbour Board Wharf Offices and Woolstore; in the 1920s, it became Shed 7. The Harbour Board commissioned the building shortly after it had built the neighbouring Board Office and Bond Store (see overleaf), and again the architect was Frederick de Jersey Clere (1856–1952).

The mid-1890s iteration of Clere's practice was Clere, Fitzgerald & Richmond. Edward Thomas Richmond (1867–1896) was still on the firm's masthead in the year of his death from tuberculosis at the age of 29; the third partner was architect and engineer Gerald Fitzgerald (1857–1937). Chief Draughtsman John Sidney Swan (1874–1936; see pages 50–51) may have contributed to the design of the Wharf Offices and Woolstore, a far more decorative building than the earlier French Empire-styled Board Office and Bond Store. This time, Clere gave a neo-Classical Italianate treatment to a wedge-shaped building that curves to follow the bend of Jervois Quay and narrows at its north end to a rounded apex. Above a rusticated base with semi-circular arches, Corinthian and Doric pilasters frame the windows in a façade featuring entablatures with friezes and cornices. (Rooftop ornamentation was removed, probably after the 1942 earthquakes.) The building was to be made of Ōamaru stone; this was 'value managed' down to brick. Its most distinctive element is the oriel on its south-east corner, a perch from which the wharfinger could observe the wharves and workers. (The building was a backdrop to clashes in New Zealand's most significant industrial disputes, the 1913 General Strike and the 1951 Waterfront Lockout.) After Harbour Board assets were sold off in the 1980s, Shed 7 was converted to apartments (Fletcher Construction, 1994).

Wellington Museum
(Harbour Board Office and Bond Store)

2–3 Jervois Quay and Queens Wharf

Frederick de Jersey Clere, 1892
Historic Place Category 1

From its establishment in 1880 until its dissolution in the
1980s, the Wellington Harbour Board was responsible for the
development and operation of the city's port. For nearly all of those
years the organisation was based in the imposing building designed
by Frederick de Jersey Clere, famously a church architect (see pages
50–51, 154–55) but evidently just as at home down by the docks.
The Harbour Board was led by eminent business figures and was
always conscious of its importance as well as its responsibilities.
The building commissioned from Clere in 1890 served as both an
office and a store where goods were kept until tax duty was paid.
The bond store had to be secure; its predecessor was a timber
building into which, as heritage researcher Rebecca O'Brien has
noted, enterprising thieves drilled to steal liquor.

Juggling the demands for architectural dignity and functional
performance, Clere designed, on reclaimed land, a three-storey
building constructed of load-bearing brick masonry on reinforced
concrete foundations and piles. The architect adapted the French
Renaissance style known as Second Empire. A distinguishing feature
of this style is the mansard roof, often with dormer windows; as
the Harbour Board building demonstrates, a mansard provides an
extra storey of space without the expense of a storey's worth of
façade. The building has typically strong French Empire massing and
a rhythmic repetition of bays and windows, but eschews the style's
heavy ornamentation, a renunciation applauded by local newspaper
The New Zealand Mail, which praised a 'practical looking building
without extravagance'. (Of course, the building looks quite fancy
to us.) After the Harbour Board was privatised out of existence, its
building was strengthened and converted by Athfield Architects
into the Museum of Wellington City & Sea (1999), which is now,
after further alterations by the same practice, Wellington Museum.

Star Boating Club and Wellington Rowing Club

Taranaki Street Wharf/Whairepo Lagoon

**William Charles Chatfield (Star Boating Club), 1886;
Clere & Richmond (Wellington Rowing Club), 1894**
Historic Place Category 1

The area around Taranaki Street wharf is like a little version of Skansen, Stockholm's famous open-air museum of buildings. Within a short stroll of each other, a collection of buildings serves up an abridged chronicle of nearly 140 years of Wellington architecture. There is work from the nineteenth century and the early twenty-first century, from the Art Deco decades and the 1960s; there's an echo of Post-modernism, an essay in cultural symbolism and even, in the façade of the Circa Theatre building, a cruel case of Baroque Revivalist amputation.

The past is most evidently present in the two Victorian-era timber buildings that sit next to each other on the eastern edge of the small Whairepo Lagoon. The northernmost of the buildings was constructed in 1886 for the rowers of the Star Boating Club, which had been founded 20 years earlier and had already moved premises twice to keep up with Wellington's harbour reclamations. Learning from these precedents, architect William Chatfield (1851–1930) future-proofed the new building, which was located on Customhouse Quay, by designing it on sleds. Just as well; only three years after it was completed, another reclamation left Star's rowers high and dry. Their clubhouse was then dragged by steam engine to a new site on Jervois Quay, where it remained for a century. In 1989, the building was relocated to its current site and put on a new foundation. Through the building's long history, the Star Boating Club has shared occupancy with a variety of groups ranging from its own Submarine Mining Volunteer Corps — a by-product of New Zealand's late nineteenth-century 'Russian Scare' — to Downstage Theatre, which performed in the clubrooms in the early 1970s.

The Star Boating Club — now called The Boatshed — has been extensively renovated over the years but essentially retains its form as a domesticated shed. It comprises a pair of long gables, running north–south, themselves centred on smaller gables facing west to the lagoon and east to the harbour. The gables are topped by finials; eave brackets are both functional and decorative; a viewing balcony extends across the west elevation of the upper pavilion level; and the frames of the large doors to the ground-floor boat storage are pitched to match the gable roof. Architect William Chatfield, who came to New Zealand as a 16-year-old, was in private practice when he designed the building, having earlier worked as a draughtsman for the Wellington Provincial Government. He had eight children and almost as many hobbies, was successful and respectable, perhaps to the point of pomposity. In 1905, he was elected by his peers as founding president of the New Zealand Institute of Architects.

The Wellington Rowing Club building, sited on the south side of the Star Boating Club, started out life as a boat house for the Naval Artillery Volunteer Corps, another outfit standing by to repel Russian invaders; that is, dressing up in uniforms for some masculine camaraderie. (The only action the militia unit saw was the invasion of Parihaka in 1881; see Te Raukura, overleaf). When constructed in 1894, the building was located at Jervois Quay, next to the Star Boating Club. The Wellington Rowing Club took possession of the building in 1931. By the 1970s, when the city council considered both rowing club buildings to be an 'eyesore in the centre of the Capital city', they narrowly escaped demolition. In 1989, the buildings were moved to their present co-location.

The Wellington Rowing Club building was restored and rotated to face the lagoon. The main features of the building are its octagonal tower — a lookout for the volunteer gunners — and the exterior boarding applied to give a half-timbered Tudor effect. A relatively complex roof of hips and gables is ornamented by finials and a pendant. The building was designed by the partnership of Frederick de Jersey Clere and Edward Thomas Richmond; stamps on archived plans also suggest the involvement of engineer Gerald Fitzgerald, who became a practice partner around this time.

Te Raukura/Te Wharewaka o Pōneke

Taranaki Street Wharf/Whairepo Lagoon

architecture+ and Mike Barnes, 2011

Numerous buildings around the Wellington waterfront testify to the colonial presence at Te Whanganui-a-Tara. Only one, Te Raukura/Te Wharewaka o Pōneke, explicitly acknowledges the history of Māori occupation. As its name indicates, the building, designed by local practice architecture+, is a whare for waka, and also accommodates a café and function centre. It is sited near what was the water frontage of Te Aro pā, a significant Māori settlement disrupted by European settlement and the 1855 Wairarapa earthquake, the largest ever recorded in New Zealand. Along with the neighbouring rowing clubhouses, Te Raukura/Te Wharewaka o Pōneke forms the eastern frame of Whairepo Lagoon, where the building's waka are launched. The rectangular building faces north-east over an ātea, the traditional courtyard space in front of the wharenui, or communal house, on a marae. At this end of the building, the decorated maihi, or bargeboards, are legible as the 'arms' of the building, in accordance with Māori anthropomorphic design principles.

The building's most striking element is its roof, a steel skin pulled down over the structure in triangular facets or folds. The analogy, introduced by Māori architect Mike Barnes, is to a korowai, or cloak, an appropriate allusion on the exposed shoreline of Te Whanganui-a-Tara. The concept resonates, too, with Te Wharewaka's praenomen: in English, Raukura means feather — korowai material, and a symbol of rank and also of the nineteenth-century peaceful resistance movement led by Te Whiti-o-Rongomai (?–1907) at Parihaka, in Taranaki, the region of origin of some Wellington iwi. On the other side of the ātea sits the bronze statue sculpted by William Trethewey (1892–1956) of the legendary navigator Kupe, his wife Hine Te Apārangi and the tohunga Pekahourangi, at the moment of their sighting of Aotearoa.

Wellington Free Ambulance Building (Former)

5–9 Cable Street and Jervois Quay

William Turnbull, 1933
Historic Place Category 1

Uniquely among New Zealand cities, Wellington's ambulances are not run by the St John's organisation, and nor is there a charge for their use. The Wellington Free Ambulance was founded in 1927 by then-Mayor Charles Norwood (1871–1966), the local agent for several carmakers — in twentieth-century New Zealand, an exclusive automobile franchise was a licence to print money — and a prominent philanthropist, as was his wife, Rosina. The new ambulance service was originally consigned to the old Naval Artillery Boat Shed (now the Wellington Rowing Club; see pages 28–31), but Norwood, overcoming opposition from Depression-era cost-cutters, raised money for a 'distinctive, modern and functional' building that would garage 10 ambulances and provide sleeping quarters for staff.

The design commission went to William Turnbull (1868–1941), son of Thomas Turnbull (1824–1907), one of Wellington architecture's eminent Victorians (see pages 90–91, 146–49). William Turnbull, who was born in San Francisco during his family's decade-long stint in the city, was articled to his father in 1882 and partnered with him in the practice of Thomas Turnbull & Son in 1891. (William kept the firm's name after his father's death.) It seems Turnbull had intended that the Free Ambulance Building would be Classically styled and made of brick, but after the 1931 Napier earthquake he switched to the in-vogue Art Deco style and a steel-framed concrete structure. The building dignifies its purpose in its restraint and relative austerity. Turnbull gave its symmetrical form impressive clarity and leavened its mass with details such as the stepped parapets on the north and south elevations, moulding that emphasises the verticality of the window recesses, and rondels containing the cross of the order of the Knights of Malta (the Hospitallers). The building now houses a bar and restaurant.

Link Building

4 Taranaki Street

Roger Walker, 1968

It must have been a shock to the city when buildings by Roger Walker started popping up around Wellington in the late 1960s. There'd scarcely been time to come to grips with Modernism when, all of a sudden, the citizenry had to process the towers, turrets, pyramids and portholes of Walker's contemporary castles. What to make of it all? There was an ingenuousness about Walker's architecture, a tactile sense of buildings put together like portions of Lego. In the accretive nature of their assembly, Walker's houses, which might occupy half a dozen levels on a vertiginous Wellington site, alluded to the cellular compositions of the Japanese Metabolists, whose work he admired as a student. There was a suggestion, too, of New Zealand's traditional fabricator approach to architecture. And, above all, there was the exuberant expressiveness of an architect who in his own wilder way was as naturally gifted as William Gray Young, Wellington's pre-eminent inter-war architect. Where Young's teenage talent was revealed in his design of his family's house, Walker's precocity was demonstrated in 'Fort Nyte', the multi-level hut he made from builder's off-cuts in the backyard of his family's house in 1950s suburban Hamilton that got so big it attracted the attention of the city's planners.

The little Link Building on the Wellington waterfront was commissioned by the Harbour Board as a customs tollhouse and designed by Walker when he was working for the firm of Calder, Fowler, Styles & Turner. It looks like a shard of a larger Walker building. Typically, it is constructed of white-painted concrete block with a steeply pitched metal roof. Projecting windows provided the building's occupants the surveillance outlook of a ship's bridge. The building, now used by the ambulance service, served for years as a diving platform for those brave enough to launch themselves into the adjacent harbour basin.

Museum of New Zealand Te Papa Tongarewa

55 Cable Street

Jasmax, 1998

Given that the Dominion Museum and National Art Gallery (see pages 136–37) was completed in 1936, it's fair enough to describe its 1998 successor as a once-in-a-half-century building. Te Papa, as the Museum of New Zealand Te Papa Tongarewa is always called, may turn out to be more than that. It will be a long time before Aotearoa New Zealand again tries to come up with a singular building to tell the country's stories, define its identities and exhibit its cultures. Public museums are high-stakes projects anywhere, but can be particularly fraught in a small country where so much is invested that too much is expected. More than most buildings, Te Papa is a monument of its moment — culturally, architecturally and museologically. (The exhibition philosophy controversially combined anti-elitism and Post-modern relativism.) Years of vacillation preceded the 1989 competition to choose Te Papa's architect. Bicultural awareness was a selection criterion; few, reportedly, of the 37 entries, especially those involving overseas architects — including Frank Gehry (pre-Guggenheim Bilbao) — revealed 'an understanding of cultural realities in this country'.

Auckland-based Jasmax won the competition, and designed a six-storey, 36,000-square-metre building, base-isolated on reclaimed waterfront land. Architects Ivan Mercep (1930–2014) and Pete Bossley sought to express biculturalism at a level beyond formalism or decoration. Reference to settlement patterns generated a Māori orientation, towards the sea and the open landscape, and a Pākehā or European orientation towards the colonial city. But the big building has an ambivalent relationship with both its maritime site and its urban connection, although the latter has been helped by Waitangi Park (Wraight Athfield Landscape + Architecture, 2006). Te Papa had to give so much to the nation; perhaps it's not surprising it had little left over for the city.

Wakefield Street Apartments

276–284 Wakefield Street and Blair Street

Architecture Workshop, 2002

Wellington has never had enough flat land to build on. No sooner had the settlers disembarked from their ships than they started filling in the harbour, almost as energetic in their 'reclaiming' of the sea as they were in their claiming of the land. Even so, building lots near the city centre remained at a premium. At the start of the twenty-first century the disequilibrium between supply and demand was heightened by an increased appetite for urban living. In response, developers and architects looked up and found higher ground — potential building sites on top of existing buildings. Pop-up additions appeared on the central city's building stock. This new architectural type can be divided into 'compatible' additions that echo the style of the base building and add-ons that are expressly different. In both categories, the results have been mixed, but a few of the additions are excellent insertions into the city's built topography. One that works well is a group of Wakefield Street rooftop apartments.

The 'ground' for the apartments is a three-storey masonry warehouse constructed in 1906 to the design, evidence suggests, of Alfred Atkins (1850–1919; see pages 200–01). The building sits stolidly on its corner site, and its paucity of decoration — round window heads on the ground and second levels, square heads on the first floor, brackets beneath a simple cornice and parapet — makes it an ideal heavyweight plinth for the lighter-weight rooftop apartments designed by Architecture Workshop, the innovative practice founded by Chris Kelly and James Fenton. The languages of the new and old architecture are very different, but meaningful connections between epiphyte and host are facilitated by the mutual deployment of extensive glazing, and the vertical alignment of the columns of every second bay of the base with the party walls of the three rooftop apartments.

Herd Street Post and Telegraph Building (Former)

22 Herd Street

Edmund Anscombe & Associates, 1939
Historic Place Category 2

On this building Edmund Anscombe (1874–1948) demonstrated his big-scale dexterity with the Art Deco/Moderne styling he was using on a series of small apartment blocks in central Wellington (see pages 56–57, 66–67, 244–45). The Herd Street Post and Telegraph Building's landmark presence on a prominent site testified to the importance of the Post Office and the role of the state in the nation's economy, and was highly visible evidence of the city's post-Depression recovery. It's interesting that the Government Architect wasn't given this prestigious commission, but Edmund Anscombe had certainly earned his opportunity. His original design was for a five-storey building, with rooftop tennis courts, to house Post Office technical and accounts staff. In 1942, a sixth floor was added, apparently to facilitate secret defence communications. (No more staff tennis.)

The building sits on reclaimed land; a 1938 report in the local *Evening Post* describes the process of driving 600 concrete piles an average of 12 metres into the ground. Architectural historian David Kernohan has speculated that Anscombe's patented 'OK' cellular concrete-block system was used in the building's construction, but Heritage New Zealand's opinion is that poured concrete over steel reinforcing was a likelier structure for such a sizeable building. The thick banding that stretches around the façade, and lines inscribed in the plaster render, give a Moderne horizontality to the monolithic building. The building's virtuoso element is the main entrance on the south-west corner. The granite doorway is surmounted by a triangular oriel, which is itself capped by a Moderne roll-top, added by Anscombe when the building got its sixth floor, that swoops over the parapet. The building's mid-2000s conversion into apartments, with an extra penthouse level, raises the question of how much can be done to a building before it loses its heritage significance.

Boat Sheds

Clyde Quay Marina

William Ferguson, 1905; James Marchbanks, 1922

Terraced housing was not a common building type in early twentieth-century New Zealand, but Wellington did a nice line in terraced boat sheds. Maritime recreation — in and on the water — was increasingly popular in the city, and around the time the Te Aro Baths were built near the site of the future Freyberg Pool (see overleaf), the Harbour Board constructed a breakwater to form an adjacent marina and reclaimed land to accommodate a row of boat sheds set back against the Oriental Parade seawall. The 38 gabled sheds were built in two stages, in 1905 (sheds 2–13 and 38–49), and 1922 (sheds 14–27). All have concrete floors, walls and roofs (with a membrane cladding), and large timber doors, in matching powder blue. Some differences distinguish the two groups. The earlier sheds have recessed panels, alternately red and orange, in the walls between the doors; the later sheds have a finer roof treatment — bargeboards, in moulded concrete — and arched openings above the doors instead of the rectangular windows of the first sheds.

ROUTE 1–13

Between sheds 2–13 and 14–27 is a timber building, now housing a yacht club, built in 1943 as a hospital by the United States Marine Corps, which had a substantial presence in Wellington as it engaged in the Pacific campaigns of 1942–1944. The sheds were built by the Wellington Harbour Board, although the first tranche, at least, seems to have been drawn up by the Design Division of the city council's Works Department. These early sheds were among the last projects in the 23-year term as Harbour Board Engineer of William Ferguson, whose omni-competence and assertiveness eventually provoked political enmity (see pages 22–23). The later sheds were built by his successor, James Marchbanks, who served as Harbour Board Engineer for 24 years.

Freyberg Pool

139 Oriental Parade

King & Dawson, 1963
Historic Place Category 1

Freyberg Pool is the harbourside counterpoint to hillside St Gerard's Church and Monastery (see overleaf) and is just as much a part of the wider Oriental Bay setting. It's hard to imagine Wellington without the building, and its indispensability suggests that, in architecture, 'icons' are as likely to be the product of functional focus as heroic intent. (Although an inspirational precedent can help.) Freyberg Pool replaced the outdoor salt-water Te Aro Baths, which had been built in 1900; that facility itself succeeded barriers constructed in the 1860s to protect swimmers from the 'visits of sea monsters'. The new pool, which required some land reclamation, was designed by Jason Lewis Smith (1917–1964) of the firm of King & Dawson. Smith — Indian-born and Irish-educated — produced a building of exemplary Modernist clarity. It features a butterfly roof raised above concrete façades at its harbour and street ends — the latter punctuated by small porthole windows — and glass curtain walls on its long north and south sides. Form follows function: the roof tilts up from the pool's shallow end towards its diving board end, and in the other direction flicks up over two levels of changing and service rooms.

As critics have noted, Freyberg Pool is 'in the tradition of' a celebrated building by the Brazilian architect Oscar Niemeyer (1907–2012): Pampulha Yacht Club (Belo Horizonte, 1942). The pool is named in honour of Bernard Freyberg (1889–1963), commander of the New Zealand Expeditionary Force in the Second World War and governor-general from 1946–1952. Freyberg was also a champion swimmer. He trained at the old Te Aro Baths, and in the Dardanelles in 1915 won the first of his numerous awards for pathological valour by swimming ashore to light decoy flares to distract Turkish attention from the Allied landings at Gallipoli.

St Gerard's Church and Monastery

73–75 Hawker Street

John Sydney Swan (Church), 1908;
Clere & Clere (Monastery), 1932
Historic Place Category 1

St Gerard's Church and Monastery, a unified composition of two buildings constructed a decade and a half apart on a clifftop above Oriental Bay, is a religious site that is absolutely integral to the civic landscape of Wellington. The church was commissioned by the Congregation of the Most Holy Redeemer (Redemptorists), a Catholic missionary order, and designed by John Sydney Swan (1874–1936), who started his architectural career as a 14-year-old articled clerk in the Wellington practice led by Frederick de Jersey Clere. Swan was briefly a partner with Clere before founding his own practice in 1901 and proceeding to business and social success; his dedication to sailing culminated in his appointment as Commodore of the Royal Port Nicholson Yacht Club.

St Gerard's Church was designed in the Gothic Revival style. Built in unreinforced brick, it has a bell tower, marble altar — designed by the architect — and stained glass windows made by Hardmans of Birmingham. By the early 1930s, the busy Redemptorists required a monastery. The addition, in council-mandated reinforced concrete, with a brick veneer, was designed by Clere, architect of St Mary of the Angels (see pages 154–55) and many Anglican churches, who was then in partnership with his son, Herbert (1884–1967). Clere & Clere followed Swan's Gothic lead. The church's gabled form received a larger sibling, with a façade featuring two oriel windows. These wings bookend a three-storey Gothic Revival panoply of lancet windows, stepped buttresses and cloisters, which were later enclosed on their upper levels in deference to Wellington's winds. In the late 1980s ownership of the defining heritage site passed to an evangelical organisation. The church and monastery are now in urgent need of strengthening and rehabilitation.

'Seven Sisters'

188–200 Oriental Parade

Joshua Charlesworth, 1907
Historic Area

Wellington and San Francisco are often compared, both of them being seismic and maritime cities with old timber houses and tricky topography. One particular site justifies the comparison: the group of Edwardian houses on Oriental Parade known as the 'Seven Sisters'. There's a row of 'Seven Sisters' in San Francisco, too — the celebrated line-up of Victorian 'Painted Ladies' in the city's Western Addition district. What these septets have in common, and what explains their sibling status, is their provenance as speculative projects. In each case, the houses were a job lot. At 188–200 Oriental Parade, the developer was also the architect: Joshua Charlesworth (1860–1925).

Up-from-nothing Charlesworth understood that making real money out of architecture meant owning and selling buildings, not just designing them. Charlesworth arrived in New Zealand from Yorkshire in 1879 as an apprentice architect — he met his wife-to-be, Ellen Hallam, on the boat — and worked in the Tīmaru office of Francis Wilson (1836–1911) before moving to Auckland and then to Wellington, where, in 1887, he won the competition to design the Home for the Aged Needy. He next went to boom-time Melbourne, briefly partnering with his former boss, Francis Wilson, before completing the design of the Renaissance-style Australian Club on William Street. (The building is still extant.) Melbourne's economy crashed in the 1890s, and Charlesworth returned to Wellington. Over the next 30 years he ran a busy practice, designing scores of buildings, including Wellington Town Hall (see pages 112–13). In 1906, he leased land on Oriental Parade from the Anglican Church and designed and built eight two-storey weatherboard houses, similar in type but distinct in elements such as windows and balconies. A ninth house was added in 1909; it survives, but the house at the other end of the original row was demolished to make way for Clifton Towers (see overleaf).

Clifton Towers

202 Oriental Parade

Porter & Martin, 1963

It can be surprising, the realisation that Modernist architecture
is now old. The Clifton Towers apartment building has occupied
its Oriental Parade site for as long as the house it replaced — the
easternmost in a row of villas designed by Joshua Charlesworth
in the first decade of the twentieth century (see previous pages).
Demolition of that house left a wedge-shaped lot, with a small
reserve on its northern boundary, on which Lewis Martin (1920–
2013) designed the triangular nine-storey Clifton Towers. On each
floor there is just one apartment, nearly solid-walled at the back
but fully glazed on the sides of the building angled to face the
harbour. On these two façades, all the apartments are sheltered
from the overhead summer sun by a projecting brise soleil. These
overhangs give the building a crisp articulation and, as it heads
towards its seventh decade, Clifton Towers has kept its looks.

Clearly, Martin knew what he was doing. He had gone into
practice with former Ministry of Works architect George Porter
(1921–1998) — they had met when they enrolled at the University
of Auckland School of Architecture in 1939 — when he returned
to New Zealand from England in the early 1950s after war service
in the British Fleet Air Arm, study at London's Architectural
Association and employment in a practice specialising in hospital
projects. In the 27 years of their partnership, exemplary Modernists
Martin and Porter undertook significant design work (Martin's
responsibility) and planning projects (Porter's forte) around New
Zealand. They were both closely involved with the campaigning
Wellington Architectural Centre, helping to save Old St Paul's
(see pages 266–69) but not managing to stop Basil Spence's
Beehive (see pages 254–55). Porter was an effective, five-term city
councillor who can take much of the credit for the construction of
more than 2000 social housing units around Wellington.

Anscombe Flats

212 Oriental Parade

Edmund Anscombe & Associates, 1937
Historic Place Category 2

In the 1930s, Edmund Anscombe designed several Moderne apartment buildings in Wellington which were constructed in a burst of activity towards the end of the decade (see also pages 66–67 and 244–45). In its situation and level of amenity, Anscombe Flats was the best of the buildings. Not coincidentally — it was a personal project for Anscombe, who was the owner as well as the architect of the building.

Anscombe was nearly 60 when he bought a house on Oriental Bay in 1933. His purpose in replacing it with apartments may have been to provide income for his retirement, if he ever contemplated such — 'Work is my hobby' was his catchphrase, although the bluster was belied by his interest in motoring and golf, and membership of the Wellington Beautifying Society and the Savage Club, a men-only venue for 'rational entertainment'.

Anscombe perhaps had other reasons to build on Oriental Parade. The promenade was a place to signal success and advertise design ability, and Anscombe never sold his talent short. But family was also an important factor. The architect, who was widowed in 1923, seems to have been a very solicitous father to his two daughters. Both were unmarried when Anscombe bought 212 Oriental Parade, and one still lived with him when the flats were completed in 1937. There were four apartments in the reinforced concrete building, one per floor, each with maid's quarters attached; Anscombe tenanted three and kept one, plus the penthouse, with its office/library, den, bedroom and semi-circular sunroom — a 'masculine' environment, a women's magazine noted at the time, not that Anscombe was a playboy. Anscombe's skill and commitment to contemporaneity are evidenced in the building's Moderne marriage of horizontal lines and soft curves, its rounded windows on its sunniest corner, and column of oriel windows peeking out from the south elevation.

226 Oriental Parade

Athfield Architects, 1988

All architecture memorialises the moment of its design. Between the 1984 electoral defeat of the dirigiste Muldoon government and the 1987 stock market crash, New Zealand capitalists had the time of their lives. The shackles on the country's regulated economy were suddenly released. Wealth lost its traditional Kiwi reticence, and consumption became conspicuous. Post-modernist architecture, disruptive and meretricious, was perfect for this febrile interlude, and the style duly debuted on Wellington's most architecturally performative street.

The five-apartment building at 226 Oriental Parade was commissioned by a group of investors from the practice led by Ian Athfield (1940–2015), the larger-than-life figure who was perhaps the most notable — certainly the most identifiable — late twentieth-century New Zealand architect. The clients evidently wanted a showy building; their desire coincided with Athfield's assertiveness. By the mid-1980s, Athfield's architecture had segued from the structural expressiveness and vernacular allusions of his early career houses into Post-modernism. It seems a natural progression — playful architect meets whimsical style — but may also have been encouraged, suggests architectural historian Julia Gatley, by Athfield's encounters with the influential American Post-modernist architects Charles Moore and Stanley Tigerman. Athfield worked on the design of 226 Oriental Parade with architect Tim Nees, and his wife Clare Athfield, a designer who contributed significantly to the interior layout and material specification of Athfield Architects' projects. The most striking features of the rigorously, almost cartoonishly, symmetrical building are the two central columns on the street façade — 'Egyptian' capitals, to Gatley; 'Minoan', to another critic — and their dwarf companions. They're planters, but they could just as easily be torches. It's all very suggestive of *Raiders of the Lost Ark*; that is, Art Deco-inflected, as are the building's curved balconies, which reportedly refer to the adjacent semi-circular 1937 Bathing Pavilion and Band Rotunda (see overleaf).

Oriental Bay Band Rotunda and Bathing Pavilion

245 Oriental Parade

Wellington City Council Engineers Department, 1937
Historic Place Category 2

Colonial New Zealand loved a brass band, and to prove it more than 100 band rotundas were built in the country's towns and cities from the 1880s to the 1930s — Wellington alone had half a dozen. Swimming in the sea was another popular enthusiasm, though closely monitored, lest exposure of the flesh prove too arousing. At Oriental Bay in the mid-1930s Wellington City Council responded to both recreational constituencies, in a pragmatic exercise that revealed the changing balance of their power, by replacing an old rotunda with a bathing pavilion that could also serve as a bandstand. The building sits at the midpoint of the curve of the bay, on a concrete platform on the harbour side of the seawall constructed after the First World War.

The pavilion was commissioned by the council in 1935 but was delayed by a jurisdictional squabble with the Harbour Board and protests from local residents worried about losing their view. In 1936, the existing wooden rotunda was removed to a suburban park and construction began. The building was designed by the council's own engineers. It's not clear whether an architect was involved. If not, it didn't matter: the pavilion had a sturdy grace. The form of the single-storey reinforced concrete structure followed the shape of its semi-circular base. The pavilion's disc-like appearance — to keep the neighbours happy, it rose only 1.7 metres above the footpath — emphasised the horizontality of its Art Deco styling ('ablutional Moderne', in one critic's description). Steps led up to the flat roof — an open-air space for viewing and music making — and down to the beach; glazed windows admitted light into the changing rooms. Fifty years later, an upper level housing a restaurant was added (Sinclair Johns Partnership, 1985). The latest restoration and renovation started in 2021.

Sunhaven

262–264 Oriental Parade

Alfred Victor Smith, 1940

By the end of the 1930s, the eastern side of Oriental Parade was substantially built up and the promenade was well on its way to securing its status as Wellington's most glamorous street. At Oriental Bay, apartment living had caught on, and so had apartment renting — deviations, both of them, from New Zealand's traditional domestic norms. Sunhaven, to judge from the flurry of classified ads that appeared after its construction, was designed with the rental market in mind. The Moderne styling of the six-storey reinforced concrete building — flat roof, horizontal stripes around the parapet, balconies with curved corners and rolled steel handrails — promised a level of contemporary amenity that the apartments delivered: garages and an electric lift; kitchens with a refrigerator; bathrooms with a shower. The five street-front apartments have the expensive views but at the rear the building shuffles sufficiently sideways to offer the other six flats some prospect of the bay. On the building's south elevation, the windows are angled to grab some light and outlook to the wider scene.

Sunhaven doesn't have the finesse of the Anscombe Flats, a similarly scaled predecessor further along the Parade (see pages 56–57), but it contributes congenially to the streetscape. The building was designed by Alfred Victor Smith (1888–1979), who was born in Christchurch and worked for architects in Masterton and Pukekohe before enlisting in the Auckland Mounted Rifles in 1914 and serving at Gallipoli. When he returned from the war, Smith set up a practice in Wellington where, over the next four decades, he reportedly designed 170 buildings. Smith doesn't seem to have been unduly handicapped by his identification with the less genteel, draughting side of the profession — he belonged to the Association of Architects & Surveyors, not the tonier Institute of Architects.

Wharenui

274 Oriental Parade

Structon Group, 1960

It's the fate of some architecture practices to be overshadowed, no matter how worthy their buildings. In New York in the 1950s the firm of Skidmore, Owings & Merrill (SOM) designed Lever House, a glass-walled skyscraper on Park Avenue, to considerable critical acclaim. Then, two blocks away, Ludwig Mies van der Rohe designed the Seagram Building, the brilliant tower that became the QED for Frank Lloyd Wright's infamous and unfair characterisation of SOM as 'the three blind Mies'. Structon Group had a SOM-ish reputation in post-war Wellington. The practice, formed in 1944 by William Edward Lavelle (1905–1974) and Ronald Muston (1905–1974), became a substantial company over the next two decades, with around 80 staff. Employing both architects and engineers, Structon was a forerunner, like SOM, of the large multi-disciplinary practice. The firm's contrived name spoke to its full-service ambition, in the service of which it was willing to sacrifice architecture's venerable auteur tradition.

Despite Structon's elevation of the collective over the 'individual genius', the design of the 10-storey, 40-unit Wharenui may be ascribed to Lavelle, or perhaps Keith Cooper (see pages 180–81). The desire to give all apartments natural light and harbour views generated Wharenui's form as a multi-faceted tower with two slightly trapezoid perpendicular wings that project forward to flank the entry lobby. This arrangement is rather awkward — as is, come to think of it, giving a private apartment complex the name for a Māori meeting house — but other design decisions allowed Wharenui to settle into Oriental Bay's mise-en-scène: it recedes from the street; it's set against the flattering backdrop of Wellington's Town Belt; it has no obtrusive ornamentation; and its off-white colour is consistent with the local palette that gives Oriental Parade its reflective dazzle. Lavelle certainly liked Wharenui; he and his New York-born wife, Margaret, lived there until their deaths in, respectively, 1974 and 1992.

Olympus

280 Oriental Parade

Edmund Anscombe & Associates, 1937

Edmund Anscombe was a vivid character, a restless, working-class autodidact bristling with purpose and possessed of an ambition that could irk his tamer professional colleagues. Anscombe was seven months old when his family arrived in Dunedin from England. He seems to have received six years of schooling before serving an apprenticeship as a carpenter, which was his father's trade. In 1888, as a 14-year-old, Anscombe made a life-changing visit to the Melbourne Centennial Exhibition. 'From then onwards,' he wrote, 'anything pertaining to Exhibitions held for me its own decided and never-ending interest.' So did travel and self-improvement. In 1901, Anscombe went to the United States, where he studied architecture — by correspondence — and worked as a builder on the celebrated 1904 St Louis World's Fair. He returned to Dunedin in 1907 and set up in practice. Over the next two decades he undertook architectural commissions in the city and throughout New Zealand. He also wrote about architecture, patented the concrete block 'O.K. Dry Wall System' and was the architect — and initiator — of the 1925–1926 New Zealand & South Seas International Exhibition. Tiring of Dunedin, he took his two daughters — his wife had died in 1924 — on a world tour in 1928–1929 and then settled in Wellington, where his career's remarkable second act included the New Zealand Centennial Exhibition of 1939–1940 and several late-1930s apartment buildings.

Dating from 1937, Olympus is a flat-roofed, four-storey building, with two apartments on each floor, designed in the contemporary Moderne style. (Anscombe was always up with the play.) The graceful linear building curves around the corner, its stripes of horizontal moulding speeding it on its turn into Grass Street, where the sheltered main entrance is framed at the base of a slim triangular column of oriel windows.

300 Oriental Parade

William Meek Page, 1930
Historic Place Category 2

Originally a four-bedroom family house but now divided into apartments, 300 Oriental Parade is almost a decade younger than its neighbour, Inverleith (see overleaf), but, if you ignore the garages, it looks much older. Welcome to the time-warping effect of the Georgian style. The Classical proportions and symmetry of the architecture of Hanoverian Britain (1714–1830) struck such a chord in the Anglophone world that scarcely had the series of King Georges (I through IV) ended than the style named for their era began its revival. For more than a century it had its devotees. Unlike the Gothic Revival, with its God-directed spires, the Georgian Revival operated on the mortal plane; it was a style concerned with expressing harmonious order in this world. Georgian architecture was prescriptive, but within the rules there was room for adjustments, and anyway, revivalism always comes with structural subterfuges that enable atavistic indulgence.

Demonstrating that you can't necessarily judge a building by its façade, 300 Oriental Parade is a concrete building behind its brick skin. There are tweaks to the Georgian type on the ground floor, which was given over to garages flanked by entrance gates, and at the top of the building, where a parapet preserves the building's horizontality by hiding its hip roof. In between, things are nicely done. White plaster friezes demarcate each floor; semi-circular arches inset with roundels distinguish the tall windows on what was the main living floor (a real piano nobile); and, cleverly, the façade gains depth by projecting by half a brick, one brick-width in from both its edges. The building's architect was Edinburgh-born William Meek Page (1881–1953), principally a designer of houses in Wellington's more affluent suburbs. The client was Sir Donald McGavin (1876–1960), an eminent surgeon and former major-general, whose impressive list of post-nominals includes the DSO (Distinguished Service Order) won on the Western Front in 1917.

Inverleith

306 Oriental Parade

Clere & Williams, 1922
Historic Place Category 2

Inverleith dates from the post-First World War period, when Oriental Parade was just starting its ascent to its status as New Zealand's best promenade. Oriental Bay's early colonial function as a convenient site for insalubrious activities, principally the boiling of whale blubber and quarantining of infectious immigrants, was almost forgotten, as was the early settlement of the area by the reputedly very unpleasant George Duppa, a land-grabber who got rich in New Zealand before returning to England and life as a country squire. By the early 1920s, a tram ran along Oriental Parade, passing swimming baths and a band rotunda. Towards the north end of the line, Francis Wallace Mackenzie (1860–1934), an Otago-born doctor who had served with the British army in the Sudan and a New Zealand contingent in the South African War, and his Scottish wife, Susan (1860–1938), commissioned an apartment building — Oriental Parade's first — from the firm of Frederick de Jersey Clere and Llewellyn Edwin Williams (1884–1967).

Inverleith, presumably named for the Edinburgh suburb, is a five-storey building, one apartment per floor, plus a rear cottage, constructed in steel-reinforced concrete with a stucco finish. Like much of Oriental Parade, the building is happily heterodox in style; the street's sunny aspect seems to encourage architectural playfulness. Under a Classical cap of cornice and dentils, Inverleith's façade is bifurcated vertically into a convex column of bow windows and a flat stack of arched windows. (The latter, which serve the apartments' sunroom, gained balconies in 1994.) Inverleith's disposition belies the drama occurring around the time of its construction. In 1920, in a sensational court case, Dr Mackenzie was struck off the medical register for three years for conspiring with the 'seducer' of a young woman to abduct her from her father, who allegedly intended her to have an abortion.

ROUTE 2:
TE ARO FLAT

CIRCA 3 KILOMETRES

The blocks west of Kent and Cambridge Terraces and south to Te Ngākau Civic Square constitute a part of the city given over to what planners call 'mixed use'. In other words, the neighbourhoods have some grit and texture. Commercial activities range from car yards to restaurants, and cultural venues include a theatre, art gallery and playhouses. The architecture of this area of atypically flat land — some of which was heaved up in the 1855 earthquake — is an eclectic mix of styles from the early twentieth century and the Modern era. Around Te Ngākau Civic Square several mid-century Modernist buildings keep company with the Classical Town Hall, Brutalist Central Police Station and Post-modern library. This route includes hotels, religious buildings and Wellington's School of Architecture. It also visits the remnant enclave of Wellington's Chinatown, and humanly scaled Cuba Street, which over the past two decades has become the Bohemian centre of the city.

Central Fire Station

2–38 Oriental Parade

Mitchell & Mitchell, 1937
Historic Place Category 2

Moderne architecture has some associations that are reputationally problematic. One is its close relationship to Art Deco — it's often hard to say where one style stops and the other starts — and Art Deco is a style that excites strong feelings, for and against. The other is its identification with the 1930s, a decade which had, shall we say, many issues. Another factor that bears on Moderne's status is the style's occurrence as a post-Beaux-Arts interlude before the triumph of Modernism. Gramsci's aphorism from 1930 comes to mind: 'The old is dying and the new cannot be born; in this interregnum a great variety of morbid symptoms appear.' All this said, you can see the attraction of the Moderne style to architects asked to design important civic buildings. The style is serious but not severe. It doesn't have the uncompromising, hard-edged clarity that glass curtain-wall Modernism would bring, but it's a long way from the sententiousness of the Baroque Revivalism that was still being realised in Wellington as late as the 1920s (see Parliament House, pages 256–57).

The practice of Mitchell & Mitchell, led by Cyril Hawthorn Mitchell (1891–1949) and his brother Allan Hawthorn Mitchell (1905–1973), used the Moderne style in designing Wellington's Central Fire Station, the building that impressively marks the eastern boundary of the CBD and terminates at Oriental Parade. The Fire Station, which opened in 1937 and is still the Wellington Fire Service headquarters, had room for nine appliances and quarters for 21 married couples and 33 single men; it had a billiard room, gymnasium, library and tennis courts. Centred on a clock tower, the three-level building is rigorously symmetrical. Two plainer ends flank a middle core featuring pilasters and a frieze above the five appliance doors. Other façade elements, picked out in darker colours, include horizontal and vertical mouldings, a stepped parapet with an acroterion, and two rondels (with flames).

Embassy Theatre

11 Kent Terrace

Llewellyn Williams, 1924
Historic Place Category 1

There was quite a bit of toing and froing of architects across the Tasman in the decades before the Second World War. One Australian architect practising in Wellington in this period was Llewellyn Edwin Williams (see also pages 236–37). Williams was born in Sydney and worked for his father — an architect who had started out as a stonemason — before studying in London. He arrived in Wellington in 1916 and went into business with Frederick de Jersey Clere, a serial monogamist, professionally speaking, whose practice partnerships did not always end amicably. Williams formed his own practice in 1919, and a few years later was commissioned to design a picture theatre by Robert Kemball (1881–1969), a one-time Masterton butcher who was rapidly — and, as it turned out, unsustainably — building a national cinema chain. Kemball spent hugely — £100,000, it's said — on the construction of what was originally called the Theatre de Luxe, a four-storey reinforced concrete building sited on the busy corner where Kent Terrace faces Courtenay Place.

The 1800-seat theatre, which opened on 31 October 1924 with a gala showing of Cecil B. DeMille's *The Ten Commandments*, was described as 'neo-Greek' in style. On the façade that fronts the big box, Williams deployed columns, a frieze of urns and shields, rondels, and a parapet with acroteria. The building certainly speaks the same language as the later Central Fire Station (see previous pages). After the fall of the Kemball theatre empire, the de Luxe — renamed the Embassy — steadily declined until it was restored by a trust and the city council, which now owns the building. Llewellyn Williams returned to Australia in 1940. His son John, who was born in Wellington, was an Australian air ace executed by the Gestapo after participating in the 1944 'Great Escape' from Stalag Luft III prisoner-of-war camp in Silesia.

Hannah Playhouse

12 Cambridge Terrace

James Beard, 1973

The post-war generation of architects in Wellington have received some academic attention but not the wider appreciation they deserve. This may be because their era generally wasn't that exciting compared to the decades on either side of it. More particularly, the architects who came of age in the 1940s and 1950s were serious Modernists. They weren't working with the more familiar, less challenging styles deployed in the city by predecessors such as William Gray Young and Edmund Anscombe and they did not exhibit the personal and professional flamboyance of successors such as Ian Athfield and Roger Walker. Many of the city's architects in this period also worked in relative anonymity, as staff members in the Government Architect's office of the Ministry of Works (MoW).

One architect who worked for the MoW and came out the other side was James Beard (1924–2017). Beard was also an urban designer before the term had currency in New Zealand and he made a huge contribution in this field. After his MoW stint, he studied planning at Massachusetts Institute of Technology and landscape architecture at Harvard University's Graduate School of Design, where he later worked as a research assistant. Beard was for a short time part of a super-group of Wellington Modernist architects that also included Allott Gabites (1919–2004), William Toomath (1925–2014) and Derek Wilson (1922–2016), before setting up his own practice. In the early 1970s he squeezed the Hannah Theatre onto a tough, rhomboid-shaped corner site. In collaboration with theatre designer Raymond Boyce (1928–2019), Beard designed a seven-storey Brutalist building in 'off-form' or 'off-shutter' concrete, with an asymmetric roof to accommodate set changes and lighting gantries. 'My idea,' Beard said, 'was for quite a rugged thing so they could do anything in the space and bash it about.'

Cambridge Terrace Post Office (Former)

21–23 Cambridge Terrace

John Thomas Mair, Government Architect, Public Works Department, 1930

Like the nearby Embassy Theatre (see pages 76–77) and Central Fire Station (see pages 74–75) the Cambridge Terrace Post Office building dates from that transitional inter-war period in which New Zealand architecture was edging towards Modernism. It's understandable that Art Deco and its Art Moderne variant were popular styles. Buildings designed in these styles looked contemporary but they weren't revolutionary. In their detailing and symmetrical massing, they provided reassurance to a public familiar with the ordering and ornamentation of the various revivalisms — Gothic, Classic, Baroque — that had played out in New Zealand cities over the previous 70 years. Those styles used a fair amount of legerdemain in their presentation of columns, pilasters and entablature as structural elements. Art Deco and Moderne architecture also deployed Classical tropes from the Beaux-Arts box of tricks but in the thinner medium of motif.

The Cambridge Terrace Post Office exemplifies Art Deco's historicist twist on modernity. The building, which is now a backpackers' hostel, was designed by the Government Architect John Thomas Mair (1876–1959). Mair was first employed in an Invercargill practice; he then worked in Wellington for the Railways Department and Thomas Turnbull & Son before attending the Beaux-Arts-oriented School of Architecture at the University of Pennsylvania. His subsequent long service to the state — he was Government Architect from 1923 to 1941 — was distinguished by his decency and sense of duty. Mair's design for the Cambridge Terrace Post Office declared the building's civic importance. Vertical emphasis was achieved by flanking an eight-storey central section with stepped back six-storey wings; street-level impact was achieved with an arrangement of four pilasters with Ionic capitals, surmounted by an architrave, frieze, cornice and coat of arms.

Elliot House

43 Kent Terrace

William Gray Young, 1913
Historic Place Category 1

As an architect, William Gray Young (1885–1962) was a natural. He wasn't flash or flamboyant, expensively educated, extensively travelled or particularly original, but he was highly competent, very focused and well organised. He was 17 when the house he designed for his parents in the new Wellington suburb of Kelburn was built. His family seems to have been comfortable but only recently middle class — his father was an immigrant watchmaker turned jewellery shop owner. After high school, Young took evening classes while articled to the firm of Crichton & McKay. He was 20 when he won third prize in a competition for workers' houses in the Wellington suburb of Petone — four were later built, to his design — and a year older when he won the competition to design Knox College in Dunedin. He started his own practice the next year.

In 1923 Young, with his brother Jack (1887–1967) and Hubert Morton (c1896–1965), established Gray Young, Morton & Young, which in the 1950s morphed into Gray Young, Morton, Young, Calder & Fowler. By the time he retired, a month before his death at the age of 77, Young had been involved in the design of, it's claimed, around 500 buildings (see, for example, pages 194–95, 200–01, 218–19, 224–27), mainly in Wellington and most of them houses. He admired the Georgian style, and in 1913 employed it on a home and surgery for James Elliot (1880–1959), then in the early stage of an eminent medical career. Even in its altered state — see the added dormer windows — the concrete-reinforced brick house stands out amid the junkspace of Kent Terrace. A symmetrical five-bay façade, edged with quoins of projecting bricks, centres on a doorway crowned with a semi-circular pediment. Windows are segmentally arched on the ground floor, square-headed on the upper floor, and timber dentils decorate the wide eaves.

Moore Wilson's Warehouse

Corner of Tory and College Streets

Athfield Architects, 1985

Being the nation's capital has been enormously beneficial to Wellington, which, apart from its location at the mid-point of the country, has few natural advantages to offset the handicaps of its climate, topography and seismic vulnerability. The pluses of its capital status are tens of thousands of relatively well-paid civil service jobs — the corporate head offices that once clustered in Wellington have mostly relocated to Auckland — and the presence of prestigious cultural institutions, such as the national museum, national library, national orchestra, national ballet, et cetera. Of course, the downside of fortunate plenitude is complacency, and there was a sense in the later decades of the twentieth century that Wellington had become dull. You know your city has a vitality deficit when its most conspicuous street life is the 5 p.m. stampede of cardiganed commuters to suburban trains.

In the years before Wellington's reinvention, via the early 1990s 'Absolutely, Positively, Wellington' branding campaign, and the city's subsequent *Lord of the Rings* idyll and its apotheosis as 'coolest little capital', it fell to architecture to provide some civic brio. From the middle of the 1960s to the start of the 1990s, Ian Athfield and Roger Walker provoked Wellingtonians with their vernacular-inflected Post-modernist buildings. In these years, the architects mainly designed houses, but they also attracted commercial clients wanting something different. The director of grocery business Moore Wilson's had seen supermarkets in the United States designed for the small BEST chain by Sculpture In The Environment (SITE), a New York-based practice led by architect and conceptual artist James Wines. BEST supermarkets had crumbing walls and distressed façades, which were variously interpreted as kitsch or a commentary on consumer culture. Athfield Architects applied a SITE-like treatment to Moore Wilson's store, tilting an office extension (since removed) and cracking a boundary wall to add a coda of seismic unease to a Post-modernist prank.

Wellington Chinese Masonic Society Building

23 Frederick Street

Architect unknown, 1925

Trying to make a new life in an unsympathetic place in the decades around the turn of the twentieth century, Wellington's Chinese population turned to mutual aid societies that connected them to China's history and their ancestral regions. One of these societies was the Chee Kung Tong — the 'Society for the Public Good', in Cantonese — an organisation with origins in the seventeenth-century resistance to the Qing rulers who had overthrown the Ming dynasty. The legacy of this resistance was strong in the southern province of Guangdong ('Canton'), the source of much of the Chinese migration to New Zealand (and Australia and North America). The Chee Kung Tong was established in Wellington in 1907. In 1919, the tong — or association — adopted the name Wellington Chinese Masonic Society, perhaps because 'tong' was a term that fed paranoia about 'secret societies'.

By the mid-1920s, the Chinese Masonic Society had accumulated the resources to construct a building on Frederick Street. It's a simple, rather Classical, two-storey unreinforced masonry structure, with a symmetrical façade featuring square pediments above the door and upper-floor windows, and a narrow balcony across the width of the building. The distinguishing elements are the Chee Kung Tong characters raised in relief and framed in the centre of the upper level and the Masonic compass symbol still discernible on the parapet. The building's opening in October 1925 evidenced civic good will — the mayor was present and complimentary — or at least a willingness to give the Chinese Masonic Society the benefit of the doubt. Former government minister and long-time mason George William Russell told the audience he 'did not know about the principles of the Chinese Order, but trusted they had their Great Architect of the Universe'. New Zealand branches of the Chee Kung Tong were disbanded in 1975, and the Wellington Chinese Masonic Society building was sold in 1982; it could do with some care.

Chinese Mission Hall

40–46 Frederick Street

Frederick de Jersey Clere, 1906

From the late nineteenth to the mid-twentieth century a couple of blocks between Tory and Taranaki Streets invoked suspicion and fascination in the wider city. In those decades, Haining Street and Frederick Street and their associated alleyways constituted the heart of Wellington's Chinatown, or as local newspapers often put it, the 'Celestial quarter'. The little neighbourhood had its own businesses, societies, customs and particular pastimes; its dynamic would have been familiar to any people down through the ages who have been compelled to stick together and then blamed for their otherness. A Chinese population formed in Wellington after the South Island goldfields were exhausted and made the best of things despite government measures such as the imposition of a poll tax, introduction of warrantless police searches, ban on female immigrants and denial of old-age pensions and family allowances. The press ran titillating accounts of Chinatown opium and vice, but the most sensational story to come out of Haining Street was the 1905 murder of a frail ex-miner by a racist English psychopath. For all the whipped-up hostility, though, you get the impression that many non-Chinese Wellingtonians weren't averse to visiting Chinese shops or using Chinese medicines or enjoying the frisson of a game of pakapoo after the pubs had shut.

One organisation prepared to reach out to the Chinese community was the Anglican Church, which partnered with the community in commissioning a building on Frederick Street to serve as a church and meeting hall. Frederick de Jersey Clere designed a simple brick Gothic Revival building with a gable above the parapet, another above the door, and lancet windows. A five-pointed star at the building's apex is the only decoration. Tenders for the hall's construction were invited in October 1905; the building opened in March 1906. It has been empty for many years.

Wesley Methodist Church

75 Taranaki Street

Thomas Turnbull, 1880
Historic Place Category 1

In short order at the peak of his career Thomas Turnbull designed churches for three of the city's main Protestant denominations. Turnbull's trinity of holy buildings, located less than a kilometre apart at the south end of the city centre, comprised churches for the Anglicans (1879; see pages 146–47), Presbyterians (1885; see pages 148–49) and Methodists. (William Crichton deprived Turnbull of the complete Protestant set when he designed the Baptists' 1895 church, which is no longer extant.) The church Turnbull designed for the Methodists, which was built in 1880, was the Wellington Wesleyans' fourth attempt in 40 years to establish a permanent home. A rudimentary early structure was replaced by a church on the corner of Manners and Cuba Streets; that was destroyed by an earthquake in 1848, and its successor was also an earthquake casualty, this time in 1855. The next timber church burned down in the 'Great Te Aro Fire' of 15 June 1879. Someone, perhaps, was trying to tell the Methodists something; if so, they listened, and acquired a new site large enough to gain exemption from the city council's post-Te Aro fire requirements for masonry or concrete boundary walls.

Although an able exponent of the Gothic Revival style, Turnbull was hardly purist in his approach, certainly in comparison to his great Christchurch contemporary, Benjamin Mountfort (1825–1898). Constructed of rusticated kauri weatherboards on a timber frame, Wesley Methodist Church combines Gothic gables, pinnacles, spires, buttresses and quatrefoil windows with Classical rounded arches above doors and windows. There's a suggestion of Norman architecture in the square, slightly projecting towers flanking the entrance, and even a hint of Venetian Gothic in the tracery of the large window that is the centrepiece of the building's main façade. Inside, an elliptical ceiling, spanned by kauri ribs, echoes the curved shape of the auditorium.

Skybox

26 Egmont Street

Gerald Melling, 2001

Gerald Melling (1943–2012) was a Liverpool-born architect who came to Wellington in the 1970s and built a unique career in the city. He was a writer — a critic, architectural biographer and poet — as well as an architect, and he pursued his vocations in tandem for 40 years. He was brought to New Zealand by the Ministry of Works (MoW), which recruited many architects from Britain in the 1960s and 1970s. Melling and the MoW was not a happy marriage, but at least it was a short one. If the men from the Ministry had seen any issues of *Satyrday*, the Toronto underground magazine Melling edited in the late 1960s, they would have realised he was, as he later confessed, 'nobody's soldier'. The Institute of Architects made this discovery in the 1980s when they appointed Melling as editor of their journal, *New Zealand Architect*. Melling told the Institute he would introduce criticism into the publication; when he did, not everyone was happy about it. His tenure as editor ended in recriminations, accompanied by lawsuits.

Melling cared about what he did. When he escaped the MoW he worked for the Wellington Education Board, producing innovative, child-focused designs for half a dozen primary schools. Later, he designed, and helped build, 50 houses in Sri Lanka for villagers displaced by the 2004 tsunami. Through the 1990s and 2000s, when he practised in partnership with Allan Morse, Melling designed, and became synonymous with, a series of 'boxes', clever, economical houses such as the Music Box (1996) for a cellist, the Samurai Box (2004) for a martial arts teacher and the Signal Box (2007), beside a Wairarapa railway line. And there was also Melling's own 'box' — the multi-level, gravity-defying, somehow-council-approved Skybox (2001), occupying the airspace above the Melling:Morse office, perched above a little outlaw lane in which the architect felt right at home.

Theosophical Society Hall

19 Marion Street

Architect unknown, 1918

All New Zealand cities have an ecclesiastical geography. Churches were part of the colonial package, explicitly in the planned settlements of Christchurch and Dunedin and as a matter of course everywhere else. In most towns the Church of England, as the establishment church, had first pick of the desirable building sites and the other mainline Protestant denominations and the Catholics contested for the rest. But that wasn't it, as far as the religious landscape went. In the later nineteenth and early twentieth centuries new spiritual movements — the New Age religions of their time — sprang up, especially in America, and gained adherents in New Zealand. By the time these groups came to build gathering places, the prime urban sites were taken. So the congregations established themselves in city fringe areas. And there they still are, the Spiritualists, Rosicrucians, Seventh-day Adventists, Builders of the Adytum and Theosophists. The latter movement, which had been founded in New York in 1875 by Helena Petrovna Blavatsky, was locally boosted by visits to New Zealand in 1894 and 1908 by Annie Besant, the English social reformer and global phenomenon who was the British Empire's most famous Theosophist. The sorrows and senselessness of the First World War may also have aided Theosophist recruitment.

The Theosophists' Wellington hall, which opened in 1918, was probably designed by its unknown builder — the surviving plans are rudimentary — under Theosophical Society direction. It presents to the street as a small Greek temple, albeit one with two porthole windows. Four Doric pilasters are surmounted by a simple entablature and a triangular tympanum bearing Theosophy's motto — 'There is no religion higher than truth' — and the Society's seal, composed of an ouroboros (tail-swallowing serpent); intersecting triangles; ankh (the Egyptian symbol of life); the Sanskrit symbol for Om (the sacred word); and a swastika, the whirling cross that symbolises creation.

Schools of Architecture and Design

Victoria University of Wellington, 139 Vivian Street

Craig Craig Moller, 1994

For an architect, being asked to design a school of architecture is quite a compliment, but it's also an offer that comes with risks attached. Your work will be evaluated immediately by academic staff and for years after by generations of students. Gordon Moller is not one to shy from a challenge, however; his career output includes New Zealand's tallest building, Auckland's Sky Tower, completed in 1997. Earlier in the decade, Moller, then a director of the practice Craig Craig Moller, was the lead architect, working closely with project architect Guy Cleverley, on the design of a building for Victoria University's School of Architecture. (The university's School of Design Innovation also occupies the building.) The school had decamped from the university's Kelburn campus in a controversial move that raised — and seemingly answered — some questions about the place of a professional discipline such as architecture within the academy.

From a sustainability perspective, the school's new home is admirable. Moller and his colleagues were briefed to convert a 1970s warehouse, located in the Vivian Street red-light district, into a teaching facility, and given less than a year and a half to do it. The architects also project-managed the job, a state of affairs inconceivable in today's construction sector. Moller added a 3000-square-metre floor to the existing three storeys, put in massive diagonal braces at ground level, and bifurcated the building with a glazed insertion housing a full-height atrium. Throughout the interior, inexpensive materials — galvanised steel and aluminium, plywood and steel mesh — reinforce the semi-industrial aesthetic. The building is a memento of its moment, a fusion of residual Modernism, 'serviced shed' High-tech and Deconstructivism, with a dash of Post-modern whimsy courtesy of the curved parapet and promiscuous paint colour.

National Bank, Te Aro
(Former)

192–194 Cuba Street

Claude Plumer-Jones, c1920
Historic Place Category 1

The concrete and brick building formerly housing the National Bank's Te Aro branch, which was converted to a restaurant in 1996, is, with the Wellington Working Men's Club (see pages 104–05), the outstanding piece of Classicism on Cuba Street. Architect Claude Plumer-Jones (c1879–1938) took his lead from ancient Greece and Rome in designing a building that advertised permanence and solidity. On each of the corner building's street façades, pairs of Corinthian columns rise for two storeys from a rusticated base. Above them are an entablature and balustraded parapet. The paired columns frame tall first-floor windows treated to their own little columns and pediments in the style of a Roman aedicule, or shrine. The building's public faces were clad in imported stone — English Malmesbury stone for the base and Sydney sandstone for the upper levels. Inside, a glazed dome, 5.5 metres in diameter, soared above Corinthian columns and bank counters arranged, according to the building's initial specifications, as the ten sides of a decagon.

The National Bank's Te Aro branch was one of five around the North Island designed by Plumer-Jones during his New Zealand years. At the distance of nearly a century, the architect is an elusive character; perhaps he was in his own time, as well. The son of a London engineer, he arrived, as Claude Percy Jones, in New Zealand from Vancouver, where had been practising as an architect. This was around 1913; by the early 1920s his surname had changed to Plumer-Jones. A contemporary memoirist claimed Plumer-Jones had a strong interest in astrology and incorporated signs of the Zodiac in his buildings, which opened on auspicious dates. (Were National Bank managers also astrologists?) Plumer-Jones seems to have left New Zealand towards the end of the 1920s; he died some years later in England.

Albemarle Hotel

59 Ghuznee Street

James Bennie, 1906
Historic Place Category 2

The Edwardian years were a time of growth and increased prosperity in Wellington, and one sign of the confident times was a building boom in the Cuba Street neighbourhood. In 1906, the 31-room Albemarle Hotel was constructed on Ghuznee Street; the building is still there, having certainly done its bit to contribute to the social history of the city. The Albemarle was built as a 'private hotel' that could provide accommodation but was not licensed to sell alcohol. It was designed by James Bennie (1873–1945), who arrived in New Zealand from Scotland as a child and grew up on the West Coast. Bennie received his architectural education at the Working Men's College in Melbourne and then practised for a number of years in Greymouth before moving to Wellington. Over the next three decades he designed more than 200 buildings, the most notable being the spectacularly ornate Hotel Arcadia (1905), demolished in 1938 to make way for the State Insurance Building (see pages 188–89).

The concrete and brick Albemarle was less fantastic, but still fruity. Doric columns on the ground floor, flanking the arched doorway and windows, are continued by foliated Corinthian columns on the first floor and plain columns with Corinthian capitals on the second. An octagonal tower is capped with a cupola. In its early days the Albemarle had a working-class clientele; during the 1913 Great Strike, the hotel was the unofficial headquarters for the striking unionists. For many years the Albemarle was one of several boarding houses owned and operated by Clara Hallam (1885–1976), who rented out rooms by the hour and accepted alcoholics as tenants, when few others would. 'Ma Hallam' also let some of her better rooms to police officers, which didn't stop her getting imprisoned in 1943 for running a 'house of ill-fame'. The Albemarle is now being restored.

Cadbury Brothers Building

60 Ghuznee Street

Hoggard & Prouse, 1909

The British Empire has long since marched into the sunset, but the echo of its presence is still discernible in New Zealand's capital city. One imperially resonant route is Ghuznee Street, an early example of the colonial habit of naming places after British military adventures. Here, the incident being memorialised was the attack on the city of Ghazni — Ghuznee is a transliteration — during the 1839 British invasion of Afghanistan led by the Governor-General of India, Lord Auckland, who got a whole New Zealand city named after him. (You do wonder how long it will be before place names signifying slaughter are replaced by more edifying titles.)

The Cadbury Brothers Building also has imperial connotations, although in its case the transplanted trait was an appetite for refined sugar. The four-storey building was commissioned, and served for 60 years, as an office and warehouse for the Cadbury family's Birmingham chocolate manufacturing company. In Edwardian times, warehouses may have been as utilitarian as they ever were, but they sure were treated to some fancy façades. The particular delights of the steel-framed Cadbury Building are the Romanesque arches and windows on the second floor, supported by brick piers rising from the floor below, and the striped columns — candy canes, anyone? — projecting from the third level. An arched parapet is the icing on this cake. The building was designed by the firm led by Jack Hoggard (1878–1936) and William John Prouse (1879–1956; see pages 152–53). Hoggard apprenticed with his uncle, William Chatfield (see pages 28–29), and worked for Joshua Charlesworth (see pages 52–53 and 112–13) before visiting San Francisco to learn about seismic-resistant steel-frame structural design. While there, he also noted the use of suspended verandahs for shopfronts and, according to his *Evening Post* obituary, introduced this building feature to Wellington.

101–133 Cuba Street

Hotel Bristol (131–133), James Gardiner, 1909;
Barber's Buildings (123–125), Crichton & McKay, 1910;
Wellington Working Men's Club (101–117),
Thomas Turnbull & Son, 1904, 1908
Historic Place Category 2

Cuba Street is just far enough removed from the corporate and government heart of Wellington's CBD to have escaped the developer attention that reshaped many parts of the city from the 1970s. (The traffic planners have not been so hands-off.) The reluctance or inability of property owners to do much with seismically vulnerable heritage buildings has also contributed to Cuba Street's architectural stasis. Consequently, and to the enormous advantage of its ambience, the street has retained much of its late-Victorian and Edwardian fabric and scale. Cuba Street's two- and three-storey masonry buildings replaced earlier timber houses after electric trams started running up the street in the 1880s. Evidence of the early twentieth-century Cuba Street building boom is preserved in a group of Edwardian Classical buildings in the block bordered by Ghuznee and Dixon Streets.

The southernmost building (131–133 Cuba Street) is the Hotel Bristol (1909), designed by builder/architect James Gardiner. The symmetrical façade centres on a second-floor balcony supported on four consoles; pilasters, keystones and a segmented pediment are all present and more or less correct. Next door, at 123–125 Cuba Street, is the Barber's Buildings (1910) designed as a dye works by Crichton & McKay; its strongest and strangest feature is the pair of top-floor lunette windows that give the façade an owl-like appearance. The big sibling in this small family is the composite building stretching from 101 to 117 Cuba Street. The more ornately detailed southern half dates from 1904; the extension, featuring a large Baroque arch, was completed in 1908. William Turnbull designed the buildings for footwear magnate Robert Hannah (see pages 156–57); its name memorialises several decades of occupation by the Wellington Working Men's Club and Literary Institute.

James Smith's Department Store (Former)

Corner of Cuba and Manners Streets

Penty & Blake et al., 1907–1963
Historic Place Category 2

James Smith (1834–1902) was a Scottish draper who opened a shop in Wellington in the 1860s. He later entered into a partnership with merchant Walter Turnbull, father of the celebrated bibliophile Alexander (see pages 252–53), and at the end of the 1890s founded a retail business with two of his sons. The company survived as a family-owned entity until the 1980s. For most of its existence James Smith Ltd was synonymous with the department store at the prominent intersection of Cuba and Manners Streets. In 1921, the company bought the existing building on the site, the five-storey premises (1907) of a hardware merchant designed by Penty & Blake in the ecumenical Edwardian Free Style. A few years later the building received the first of many additions and alterations, when a steel-framed annex was added to the rear. In 1932 King & Dawson gave the original building an Art Deco makeover, introducing piers and a stepped parapet with frieze, and façade lettering in an Art Deco font. The same practice designed an addition (1934) on Manners Street; in the 1960s the building was extended down Cuba Street and seismic strengthening was carried out in the 1980s.

Until its sad demise in the same decade, James Smith's was a Wellington institution — a civic anchor, like the city's other twentieth-century department stores. Across the street is a former bank building (William Turnbull, 1913), recipient in the 1990s of one of the crudest rooftop additions in Wellington. Further down Cuba Street are three noteworthy Edwardian buildings: Nos 41–43 (1903), designed by John Sydney Swan; the Kennedy Building, Nos 33–39 (1905), by James O'Dea (c1853–1930) — note the initials on the parapet of sisters Agnes Anne and Anastasia Christina Kennedy, who commissioned the building; and Columbia Hotel, Nos 36–38 (1908), by Joseph McClatchey Dawson.

Anvil House

138–140 Wakefield Street

Kelly & Mair, 1951

Anvil House doesn't say too much, just enough to deserve attention. To get the faint praise out of the way: it is not a banal glass tower, nor a rote piece of revivalism. More positively, what explains the appeal of this Modernist building? The simple geometry of its fenestration — rows of rectangular windows and columns of small glass blocks. Its colour — chalk red, with projecting window frames delineated in white. The way the afternoon sun hits the north-facing building, communicating welcome warmth. And the building's signature gesture — the relief, low down on the front façade, of two workers hammering away. This mark, a play on the name of the building's commissioning company, Smith and Smith, and on one of its products, 'Anvil' paint, long ago lost its commercial meaning, and the sculpture is now just a graphic transliteration of the building's name. (And not, alas, as some might prefer to read it, a relic of Socialist Realism or New Zealand trade unionism's mid-century heyday.)

Anvil House was designed by the practice, active in the late 1940s and early 1950s, led by Albert Fleming Kelly (1887–1962) and John Lindsay Mair (1915–1980). Kelly attended the Marist Brothers primary school in Boulcott Street; late in life, after 40 years in practice and the death of his wife, he joined the Marist order as a lay brother at Futuna Retreat House in Karori. In the late 1950s he was passed over as architect of Futuna Chapel (see pages 270–73) in favour of John Scott. Lindsay Mair was the son of Government Architect John Thomas Mair; he was only eight months old when his mother died of tuberculosis in 1915. In the mid-1950s, Lindsay Mair was a practice partner of senior Wellington architect Vivian Haughton (1891–1956; see also pages 116–17).

Michael Fowler Centre

111 Wakefield Street

Warren and Mahoney, 1983

Michael Fowler was a partner in the architecture practice Calder, Fowler, Styles & Turner, and also a business-oriented politician with a populist bent. He served as Wellington's mayor from 1974 to 1983, campaigning as a get-things-done civic booster. In office, his focus became a new civic centre to replace the Wellington Town Hall (see overleaf). Fowler's ambition intersected with the inclinations, which might be called national culturalist, of the country's Labour government, which in 1975 offered Wellington City Council financial help to build a new hall, giving it six weeks to submit a costed design. Seizing the moment, Fowler approached Warren and Mahoney, architects of the Christchurch Town Hall (1972). Miles Warren recalls that Fowler asked for a town hall 'the same as Christchurch, only better'. Warren and his practice partner Maurice Mahoney (1929–2018) introduced raked seating and improved sightlines into the Christchurch template, and Harold Marshall developed new acoustic technologies. The main formal difference between the two buildings lies in the curvilinear treatment and raised placement of the Michael Fowler Centre's glazed circulation and foyer areas.

From the start, the Michael Fowler Centre, which has performed its functions competently, was handicapped by bad timing and poor planning. Warren and Mahoney's submission was on time but over budget; the government withdrew its support, and anyway was soon voted out of office. The project languished while Fowler chased funding, desperately and ultimately successfully. Construction finally began in 1980 but by then a public outcry had prevented the demolition of the Wellington Town Hall. Consequently, a new building intended to be viewed in the round was jammed up against an existing building, doing neither any favours. The city council, deferentially, enlisted Arthur Valerian Wellesley, eighth Duke of Wellington, to open the Michael Fowler Centre in 1983.

Wellington Town Hall

101 Wakefield Street

Joshua Charlesworth, 1904
Historic Place Category 1

It's an ineluctable law of architecture that the more important a building is at the time of its construction the greater the challenges it bequeaths to future generations. Wellington Town Hall is a heritage heavyweight. It was designed to signal its significance, built massively but weakly on reclaimed land — a problem for posterity, right there — and launched with Edwardian pomp and circumstance. The inaugural concert featured Elgar's 'Land of Hope and Glory' and a poem in praise of 'Grand Aotearoa', and the press responded enthusiastically. The usual 'chorus of cavillers and croakers' had been silenced by the revelation of a building 'superior to the more costly Sydney Town Hall', obviously a contemporary benchmark.

Wellington Town Hall was designed by Joshua Charlesworth (see pages 52–53), who won the commission in a competition in 1900. Charlesworth designed an ornately, or 'moderately exuberant', Classical three-storey building constructed in load-bearing brick on concrete foundations. The building comprised a 3000-seat concert hall (acclaimed for its acoustic quality), council chamber and offices, and large public reception room. The moulded concrete façade elements included Corinthian columns, pilasters, cornices, capitals and window pediments. The Town Hall endured in its original state for only three decades; ever since, the council has been dealing with its issues (or adding to its indignities). After earthquakes in 1931 and 1942, much of the building's exterior ornamentation was removed. Seismically motivated alterations, to the interior as well as the exterior, continued over the years; the Town Hall's style, someone said, became 'Stripped Classical, by attrition'. In the 1970s, public agitation saved the building from demolition, if not neglect, and for 50 years the council has struggled with the dilemmas of salvation. The Town Hall was closed in 2013; in 2019, the council recommitted to its restoration, which is scheduled for completion in 2024.

New Zealand Racing Conference Building

85 Victoria Street and Wakefield Street

Structon Group, 1961

Architecture's three essential virtues — from time immemorial, that is, since they were elucidated in the first century BCE by the Roman architect and engineer Marcus Vitruvius Pollio — are 'firmitas, utilitas and venustas'. Buildings should stay up, do their job and look good. In general, most big buildings in most cities, including Wellington, satisfy the first criterion and adequately meet the second. It's delight that's the difficulty, and the amount of attention paid to it reveals the level of respect given by a client and architect to the 'public realm', which means everyone else — all the people who live with a city building over the course of its life.

To an uncommon degree, the building on the southeast corner of Victoria and Wakefield Streets possesses the power to delight. It's also surprising, which can be a virtue in itself, if not a Vitruvian one. Compared to its contemporaries, the building is relaxed, even louche. Its Modernism isn't Anglo-Saxon, it's Levantine — the building looks like it's from mid-century Beirut. It was designed for the New Zealand Racing Conference, the body that supervised thoroughbred horse-racing through the twentieth century. (There's a nod to this provenance in the horseshoe motifs on the building's balustrades.) Structon Group had a generous budget for the six-storey, reinforced concrete building, as evidenced by the stainless steel and bronze sheathing and vitreous ceramic tiles, and a relatively free design hand. The commission must have been a joy for architect Keith Cooper (1926–2011). He gave the building an undulating verandah, which for 30 years has sheltered the Lido café, and a concave curve at its apex, an echo, across the years, of the façade of Gummer & Ford's Dilworth Building (Auckland, 1927). A penthouse was added in 1974; in 1987 the sharemarket crash fortuitously saved the building from demolition.

Dominion Building

78–84 Victoria Street

Crichton, McKay & Haughton, 1928
Historic Place Category 2

Curving gently to follow a bend in the road and foregrounded by alder trees and kerb-side planting that provides a buffer against traffic, the Dominion Building is a graceful interlude in Wellington's mid-city streetscape. The building was commissioned to house the offices and printing presses of *The Dominion*, the city's morning newspaper, which had been founded by business and pastoral interests and launched on the day in 1907 when the colony of New Zealand graduated to the rather ambiguous status of a British 'dominion'. The Dominion Building's seven-storey reinforced concrete structure was clad in limestone from Caen in Normandy; pressed metal spandrel panels ornamented a façade topped by a copper cupola with a lantern turret. The symmetrical design merged Stripped Classical horizontality with the Chicago School verticality expressed in the central shaft, flanking piers and slim window mullions.

When new, in the late 1920s, the building dominated its low-rise neighbourhood. Authorship was by the prolific practice founded by William Crichton (1861–1928), a Cornish immigrant whose New Zealand career began in the Colonial Architect's office, and James Hector McKay (c1866–1944), a dourly intriguing Scot who ended his architectural career in the mid-1920s to engage in serious world travel. Vivian Haughton, who had joined the practice as a draughtsman in 1907 and taken time out for war service, became a partner in the 1920s and led the firm from the end of the decade until his death. In 1976, *The Dominion* moved into a building shared with *The Evening Post*; the two newspapers, rivals owned by the same company, merged as *The Dominion Post* in 2002. In the mid-1990s, the Dominion Building was converted into lower-level commercial tenancies and upper-floor apartments by Athfield Architects. A glazed rooftop level was added, and the façade of creamy limestone, brought all the way from Normandy, was coated in green paint.

Wellington Central Library

65 Victoria Street

Athfield Architects, 1991
Historic Place Category 1

Sometimes a building is more than a building. Three decades after its construction, Wellington Central Library, a popular facility but, it turns out, a flawed structure, became the focus of a civic debate not only about its safety and utility, but also about wider issues of urban design, sustainability and heritage preservation. Wellington Central Library was designed in Ian Athfield's Post-modern phase, at a time when public libraries were being reimagined. Athfield set out to create an environment that was relaxed and engaging, and he succeeded. With its café and bookshop, exposed pipes and ducts, bright carpet and plentiful natural light, the Central Library gained fond recognition as 'Wellington's living room'. The library had city-scale work to perform, as well. It was intended to have an imposing street presence, and at the same time define an edge of Te Ngākau Civic Square, the plaza — designed by a team of architects including Athfield — that is also bordered by the Town Hall (see pages 112–13) and City Gallery (see pages 124–27). Athfield gave the building's west-facing Victoria Street elevation a staunch face of concrete panels and inset windows; the eastern façade, overlooking the square, is fully glazed. The Central Library's great populist gesture is the colonnade of nīkau palms, rendered in lead, copper and steel, along the north elevation; a smaller colonnade marks the library's entrance on Victoria Street.

In 2019, the library was closed because of the risk its precast concrete floor panels might collapse in an earthquake. A heated public discussion about whether to repair or replace the library ensued. (To every argument, a dollar figure was imputed, and duly impugned.) The matter was seemingly settled in 2021 when the city council voted in favour of rehabilitation. If this proceeds, it will cost the city upwards of $200 million.

Dominion Life Assurance Building

44 Victoria Street

Stanley Fearn, 1958

Architecture has always offered its practitioners the consolation that what they do is not just a job. It's a vocation, an all-consuming pursuit that can continue as long as passion and capacity endure. Look at Frank Gehry, in his nineties and still designing. Of course, Gehry is a 'starchitect', sitting above layers of juniors who turn his ideas into plans, using digital tools he doesn't have to understand. In the future, architects' professional longevity will depend on their success in attracting the young staff equipped to handle rapid technological change. But for three-quarters of the twentieth century, the tools and methods of architects did not change much. Styles evolved, but many architects raised in the Beaux-Arts days were able to remain sufficiently current to stay relevant. Take, for example, Stanley Walter Fearn (1887–1976), the son of a London pawnbroker who set up in practice in Wellington in 1912. The next year, he and Austin Quick designed the neo-Georgian William Booth Memorial Training College (see pages 140–41).

In the 1920s Fearn designed houses that echoed the Arts and Crafts inclinations of his mentor, the bohemian English architect Detmar Blow (1867–1939). And three decades later, he produced the Dominion Life Assurance Building, a work of Modernist idiosyncrasy as charming as the nearby Racing Conference Building (see pages 114–15) and Anvil House (see pages 108–09). Concrete-framed windows project from the façade of the nine-storey building, which is enlivened by blue tiles and Mondrian panels on the lower levels and the slim, red verandah that rises to a crown above the entrance to the building's arcade. Fearn had traditional architects' interests — golf and painting — but he also trained Amyas Connell (1901–1980), the expatriate New Zealand architect who designed a famous work of early British Modernism, the brilliant High and Over house (1931) in Amersham, Buckinghamshire.

Wellington Central Police Station

41 Victoria Street

Architectural Division, Ministry of Works, 1991

The exposed structure entered the modern architectural lexicon in 1977 with the Pompidou Center in Paris (Richard Rogers, Su Rogers, Mike Davies, Renzo Piano and Gianfranco Franchini). Locally, the technique was adapted by Warren and Mahoney when the firm deployed concrete cross-bracing as an elegant diagonal structural frame on Union House in Auckland (1984). If there was a conversation to be had about the expressive use of concrete, the Ministry of Works (MoW) — cement mixer to the nation — was not about to be left out of it. In the early 1980s, under the design direction of Gerard Hoskins (1938–2019), MoW architects began work on the new Wellington Central Police Station. It was to be one of the last MoW projects; by the time the building was completed the Ministry's Architectural Division had been corporatised, a halfway house on the short journey to complete government divestment.

The Central Police Station is a solid memento of MoW late Brutalism — a ten-storey block, with four basement levels, plus a four-storey parking building. The chunky concrete cross-bracing frees the interior of space-consuming columns and struts. More fundamentally, it adds stability to a building sitting on reclaimed land in a city sited on an earthquake fault line. The frame is integrated with a 'base isolation' system that supports the building on a foundation of reinforced concrete piles driven 15 metres into bedrock and encased in steel cylinders to separate, or isolate, them from the surrounding ground. The encased piles are topped by lead extrusion devices that act as dampers, absorbing seismic energy. From foundations to cross-bracing, the structural system provides stiffness to the building, allowing it to move as a rigid unit and enjoy a 'soft ride' in an earthquake. The Central Police Station certainly has the quality of firmness, though only a Brutalist would recognise in its staunchness a semblance of beauty.

City Gallery
(Former Wellington Central Library)

Te Ngākau Civic Square

Gummer & Ford with Messenger, Taylor & Wolfe, 1940
Historic Place Category 2

In February 1940, 500 schoolboy 'volunteers' carried Wellington Central Library's 60,000 books into their new home on Mercer Street. It was a short move at the end of a long journey for Wellington's public library, which had started out a century earlier in a raupō hut and had outgrown successive relocations before being housed in a building — soon inadequate — on the corner of Mercer and Wakefield Streets in 1893. Having eventually determined to fund a new library building, the city council ran a design competition in 1935. The two judges (this was a simpler time), long-time City Librarian Joseph Norrie (1880–1965) and Christchurch architect Cecil Wood (1878–1947; see pages 260–61), picked two winners. They liked the plan by the eminent Auckland practice Gummer & Ford but preferred the elevations drawn by New Plymouth practice Messenger, Taylor & Wolfe, so the winning firms were asked to collaborate on the design. Together, they produced a reinforced concrete building in the inter-war Stripped Classical style with a symmetrical façade, pared back but not devoid of decoration, overlooking a terraced lawn. Eight fluted pilasters surmounted by a plain entablature frame the large ground-floor windows and main entrance, and the building's edges are detailed with recessed quoins. Panels were incised with the subject areas of the library's holdings: Philosophy, Religion, Sociology, Science, Literature, Useful Arts, Commerce, Fine Arts and History.

When the Central Library opened, *The Evening Post* praised its civic contribution. It was, like its contemporaries, the National Art Gallery and Dominion Museum and Wellington Railway Station, 'one of the ornaments of a city which, in its hundredth year, shows signs of having grown up'. The newspaper's encomium was so fulsome it could have been drafted by the Institute of Architects.

'Fine buildings, like fine music and good music, work upon the minds of the people for good,' the *Evening Post* editorial continued. 'The closer one lives to fine architecture, the greater its influence.' The single improvement that could render the new library's 'charm and popularity even greater' would be the reserving of the area surrounding the building as a park 'for people, not cars'.

It was a half century before this prescient vision was realised as Te Ngākau Civic Square. As part of this development, a new public library was built in 1991 (see pages 118–19) and the existing library was converted by the council's architecture department and Stuart Gardyne into the public City Gallery. In the course of this project, the old library lost its raised terrace, but Gardyne was careful to preserve the building's original fabric. 'Tidying up the building or removing references to its previous function would deny that they ever existed,' he said. It would be 'akin to tearing out the page of a history book'. A decade and a half later, Gardyne, then a director of the practice architecture+, returned to City Gallery, designing an auditorium and new exhibition spaces contained in a resolutely modern addition — a cube, clad in rusted steel — on the building's north side.

ROUTE 3:
CENTRAL SPINE

CIRCA 3 KILOMETRES

This route starts on the edge of the inner-city suburb of Mount Cook at an elevated site — a would-be Acropolis — featuring a war memorial and a museum, and leads downhill to the middle of the city. On the way, it dips into characterful Aro Valley before heading past Gothic churches and public projects from the era of New Zealand's first socialist government, arriving at the corporate mini canyon of lower Willis Street. The route is

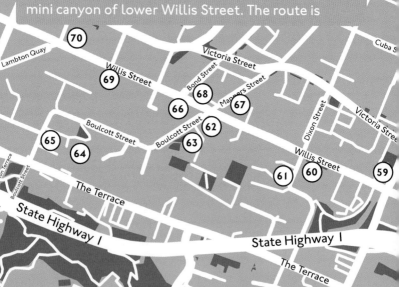

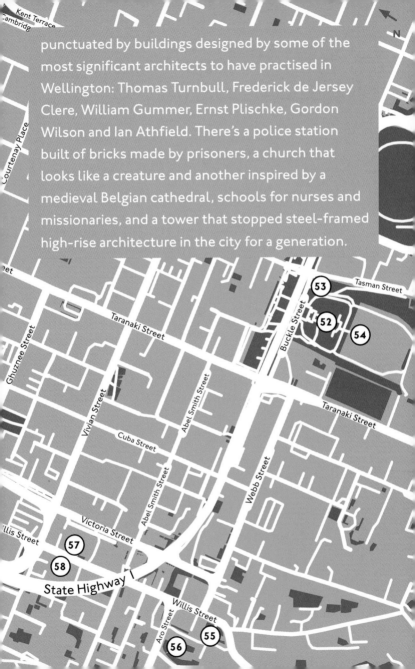

punctuated by buildings designed by some of the most significant architects to have practised in Wellington: Thomas Turnbull, Frederick de Jersey Clere, William Gummer, Ernst Plischke, Gordon Wilson and Ian Athfield. There's a police station built of bricks made by prisoners, a church that looks like a creature and another inspired by a medieval Belgian cathedral, schools for nurses and missionaries, and a tower that stopped steel-framed high-rise architecture in the city for a generation.

Carillon and Hall of Memories

41 Buckle Street

Gummer & Ford, 1932 (Carillon); 1964 (Hall of Memories)
Historic Place Category 1

The mortuary genre was a familiar architectural suffix to the twentieth century's wars. More than 18,000 members of New Zealand's armed forces died in the First World War, at a time when the population was barely one million, and as soon as the war ended the government resolved to acknowledge this 'sacrifice' — as the awful loss of life would henceforth be known — by constructing a national memorial in the nation's capital. Some indecision ensued about what the memorial should be and where it should be located. The government seems to have been spurred into action by the Wellington War Memorial Carillon Society, which in 1926 raised the money for 49 bronze bells. These were gifted to the government after they had been rejected by the rival Wellington Citizens' War Memorial Committee, which preferred a silent memorial, the Cenotaph (Grierson, Aimer & Draffin, 1932), built near Parliament House. In 1928, the government selected a site adjacent to the Mount Cook Police Station (see pages 134–35) for the national war memorial. By then, the memorial had become tied to another significant public project — the National Art Gallery and Dominion Museum (see pages 136–37). In 1929, the government staged a design competition for three structures — a carillon and associated hall of memories, and a museum/art gallery. The competition was won by the Auckland-based firm led by William Henry Gummer (1884–1966) and Charles Reginald Ford (1880–1972).

The Carillon was built first, opening in 1932. The 51-metre-high Art Deco campanile, or bell tower, rises from a rather Classical base reached via a grand staircase incorporating a brass lion's-head fountain carved by sculptor Richard Oliver Gross (1882–1964). The slightly tapered concrete tower of the campanile is mostly rendered in cement plaster; lower down it is clad in Tākaka marble. This treatment is a 1980s substitution for the original cladding of Putaruru ignimbrite, a stone which expressed the soft pink hue of Gummer & Ford's famous competition drawing, but which had endured poorly. The campanile's four façades are topped at each corner by a capital of five semi-circular copper louvres, and above that arrangement — less not being more — is a dentilled roof surmounted by a 'lamp of remembrance'. The height of the tower is accentuated by the intricately patterned, recessed concrete grilles that soar up each façade, and allow the music from the bells to escape the campanile. The bells were paid for by public subscription, cast at the London foundry of Gillett & Johnston, and named, mostly, for New Zealand's First World War battlefields. A restoration in the 1980s added some bells, including four very large base bells, and replaced others. The Carillon now has more than 70 bells, ranging in diameter from 152 to 2720 millimetres, and in weight from 4 to 12,475 kilograms. All this bronze — 30 tons in 1932, more now — has stressed the bells' supporting steel frames, and along with seismic vulnerability has presented challenging maintenance issues.

The Hall of Memories is connected to the Carillon and accessed via a vestibule in the base of the campanile. Proposed in 1929, it wasn't completed until 1964. Construction was delayed by the Depression, then the Second World War. After drawing up the hall in the late 1940s, Gummer & Ford later had to scale back the design after a change of government. The structure is concrete, but the architects managed to get away with an interior lined with Mount Somers limestone. The hall is a lovely, calm space, with a religious atmosphere generated by stained glass windows, made by French-born, London-based glass artist Pierre Fourmaintraux (1896–1974) of the English window-maker Whitefriars Glass, and recesses that suggest little side chapels, leading to an apse. But where a church would have an altar, the hall has a bronze sculpture by Lyndon Smith (1927–2003), figures of a mother and her two children, made bereft by war. It is a quietly powerful riposte to the glorification of sacrifice that is still a leitmotif of the Anzac remembrances that, every year, take place in front of the Carillon in Pukeahu National War Memorial Park.

Mount Cook Police Station
(Former)

13 Buckle Street and Tasman Street

Architect unknown, 1894
Historic Place Category 1

In the 1880s the focus of law enforcement in New Zealand started to shift from the 'frontier' to the towns; that is, from race-based to class-based policing (with some overlap, obviously). Concerns about urban unruliness loosened the purse strings of a parsimonious government and police stations proliferated. In 1894 alone, eight stations opened, one of them in Wellington's Mount Cook, an inner-city, working-class district occupying land formerly cultivated to support nearby Te Akatarewa pā. Mount Cook Police Station sits four-square on its corner site, a no-nonsense bastion garrisoned by, originally, a sergeant and half a dozen constables, with courtyard cells out the back. But it's more than that. The pattern language and construction technologies of the time, and some serendipitous manufacturing capacity, subverted what must have been a very austere brief.

The building is severely symmetrical: rounded-arch openings march along both floors, and the front door is bang in the middle of the main elevation. However: the black and white arches above the windows resemble the sleeve cuffs of antique police uniforms; the same glazed bricks wrap around the building in two thin stripes; and alternate quoins on the building's corners are stamped with a rosette. Fans of ceramic architecture will love this building. It was built by prisoners from prisoner-made bricks — Wellington's finest, produced at Mount Cook Gaol. Each header brick in the polychromatic English-bond coursework is marked with a convict arrow. It's uncertain who designed the building, but construction was supervised by Bryen Weybourne (1830–1892), Inspector of Public Works at Mount Cook Gaol and an expert brick-maker. After the station was closed in 1956 the Police Department and Dominion Museum squabbled over the building's ownership for a decade. The museum then used the building until the late 1990s; it is now a private house.

National Art Gallery and Dominion Museum

9 Buckle Street

Gummer & Ford, 1936
Historic Place Category 1

The National Art Gallery and Dominion Museum is an outstanding example of the Stripped Classical style popular with inter-war governments across the political spectrum. Another monumental example of the style is Auckland War Memorial Museum Tāmaki Paenga Hira (Grierson, Aimer & Draffin, 1929). But where Auckland's museum enjoys its site in solitary splendour and is flattered by its cladding of luminous Portland stone, the Dominion Museum is handicapped by the compromises that attended its planning and construction. Gummer & Ford's original concept placed the museum at the end of an axis extending through the Carillon and down a ceremonial boulevard to Courtenay Place. On their elevated site the buildings were presented as a little Acropolis in pink Putaruru stone. But the grande allée never happened — eventually Pukeahu National War Memorial Park (Wraight Athfield Landscape + Architecture, 2015) provided the composition with a traffic-free foreground — and the stone was, mostly, value-managed down to concrete. Consequently, the Dominion Museum was marginalised as a hard-to-reach building of grey and sombre appearance.

William Gummer's Beaux-Arts mastery, honed in the London studio of the eminent Classicist architect Edwin Lutyens (1869–1944), is evident in the rigorous symmetry of the three-storey building and especially on the stone-clad front elevation, with its colonnade of square-fluted pillars, architrave with wreaths and frieze with garlands, dentilled cornice and fretworked parapet. The line between museum and mausoleum can be fine, and the Dominion Museum's close proximity to the memorial carillon was, perhaps, not good for its health. In the late 1990s, the museum was replaced by Te Papa (see pages 38–41). The building is now owned by Massey University.

Pukehinau Flats

320 Willis Street

Burren, Keen & Fagan, c1978

A rebellious bacillus, super-spread by Ian Athfield and Roger Walker, was circulating in Wellington architecture in the 1970s. Clearly, it was highly contagious, and even a thorough grounding in Modernism provided inadequate inoculation against infection. Neville Burren (1925–1980) was an English immigrant architect who spent the first half of his New Zealand career working for the Ministry of Works (MoW). This was a period — the 1950s and early 1960s — when the state was the principal sponsor of Modernist architecture. Under the Government Architect, Gordon Wilson (1900–1959), and the head of the MoW's Housing Division, the émigré Austrian architect Frederick Newman (1900–1964), Burren designed medium-density 'Star block' public housing schemes, notably at Freemans Bay in Auckland but also in Hamilton and Wellington's new post-war suburbs.

By the end of the 1960s Burren was in private practice with Warwick Keen (1926–1985), also an ex-MoW architect. In the early 1970s, the partnership, which by then included engineer John George Fagan (1926–1985), was commissioned by Wellington City Council to design a 200-tenant housing complex for an Aro Valley site formerly occupied by the Wellington Bowling Club. Burren, Keen & Fagan organised the development as an eight-storey tower of one-bedroom apartments, and adjacent low-rise wings of two- and three-bedroom units. It's the street façade of the tower, with its array of porthole windows, that expresses the contemporary Athfield/Walker zeitgeist, although Burren and Keen had already revealed their own wild side with their design of the idiosyncratic Cuba Street Bucket Fountain (1969). The scale and design of the Pukehinau Flats attracted opposition from some of Aro Valley's new middle-class residents, as did the project's name, too close a homophone, allegedly, to 'pokey hen houses'. Town Clerk Stuart McCutcheon pointed out that Pukehinau, or the hill of the hīnau trees, was the historical term for the area.

William Booth Memorial Training College (Former)

33 Aro Street

Fearn & Quick, 1914

The Aro Valley is dank, intimate, autarkic. There are streets where the sun barely shines and chimneys smoke for most of the year. The suburb is gentrified now, but for much of the twentieth century it was a refuge for people who preferred to be out of reach or didn't have a lot of choice about where they lived. In other words, it was prime missionary territory for the Salvation Army, evangeliser to the marginalised, and an affordable location for the organisation's training college. Before the First World War, the Army bought a site on Aro Street, the valley's central thoroughfare (and one of the great Wellington streets), and commissioned a building to house 50 student officers (25 male and 25 female).

The brick and concrete building, three storeys high and organised around a central courtyard, received the neo-Georgian styling often used for collegiate architecture in the Anglophone world in the first decades of the twentieth century. On its elevated site, the building dominates the surrounding workers' cottages like a manor house lording it over an English village. The symmetrical façade centres on a stucco composition of a portico — the destination of an impressively steep stairway from the street — and four Corinthian pilasters capped by an unadorned entablature and parapet. Decorative compensation for this austerity is offered by the façade's rusticated base and corners, and the keystones set above the sash windows. The building was designed by the practice of Stanley Walter Fearn (see pages 120–21) and Austin Quick (1886–1916), which was formed in 1913 and ended when the partners went to the war; Private Quick of the Wellington Infantry Regiment is buried in a military cemetery near Armentières, in northern France. In 1982 the Salvation Army sold the building named for its founder to the School of Philosophy, which runs courses based on eastern and western traditions.

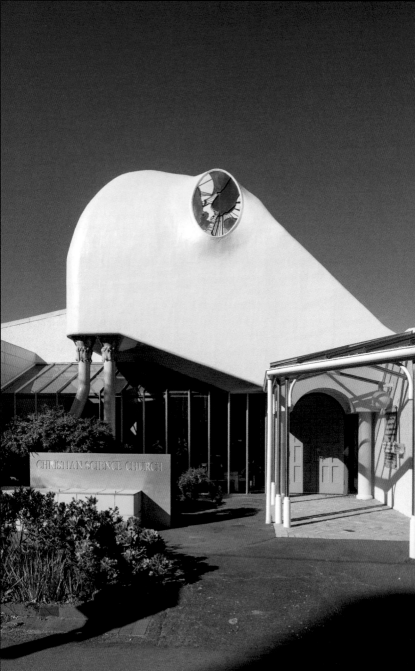

First Church of Christ, Scientist

281–283 Willis Street

Athfield Architects, 1983

In building a new church on Willis Street in the early 1980s the Christian Scientists entered a neighbourhood with strong ecclesiastical precedents. Their site was a couple of blocks from two nineteenth-century Thomas Turnbull churches, Anglican St Peter's (see pages 146–47) and Presbyterian St John's (see pages 148–49), and not far from Frederick de Jersey Clere's Roman Catholic St Mary of the Angels (see pages 154–55) — fine Gothic Revival buildings, all of them. But the Christian Scientists, having previously occupied a neo-Classical building on The Terrace, were not about to join this establishment party. Instead, they gave Ian Athfield a remarkably free hand, requesting 'a church that demonstrates the techniques of today' and is 'an identifiable place in which to worship'. Music to Ath's ears, but this open-mindedness wasn't so surprising: Christian Science, born of the revelations of Mary Baker Eddy in late nineteenth-century New England, is so non-conformist that sectarian critics dispute its Christian credentials.

Though light on liturgy, the church does hold services and the heart of the Willis Street building is a sloping, octagonal auditorium, free of the accoutrements of the Catholic and Anglican traditions, but with tilework by Neville Porteous and Clare Athfield. However, what is most 'identifiable' about the building is the form that leaps towards the street, supported on a pair of slender columns (with pink capitals designed by Clare Athfield), one of them bent out of shape. (Veterans of New Zealand's ligament-wrenching contact sports will wince at the sight of this twisted leg.) With its 'eye' window, made by glass artist James Walker (1948–2011), the cantilevered form — its function is to house the organ loft — has always invited anthropomorphic interpretation. Its spiny crest of roof steps lend the building a reptilian look; others see a whale, but my vote goes to the tuatara.

Dominion Training School for Dental Nurses (Former)

254–266 Willis Street

John Thomas Mair, Government Architect,
Public Works Department, 1940
Historic Place Category I

The building that housed the Training School for Dental Nurses for half a century continues to perform a valuable public service by providing some cohesion to a stretch of Willis Street otherwise surrendered to the traffic engineers. It's an impressive building in an authoritarian way; you can imagine a sculpted eagle perched on the cornice, or, perhaps, fasces above the main door. The style rests somewhere between Classicism — so stripped as to be almost bare — and Modernism. What distinguishes the building is the scale of the windows that march in rhythm across the top floor. These windows, 5.5 metres high, admitted natural light into an open-plan space that extended along the entire 47-metre length of the building and accommodated 49 dental stations. This was the main teaching, and largest operating, clinic of the School Dental Service, established by the government in 1921 in response to concerns about the nation's oral fitness. Two decades later, there were 300 primary school dental clinics, 'murder houses' to generations of school children.

Dental nurses were symbols of the caring state — 'missionaries of good health', Prime Minister Peter Fraser called them at the opening of the Training School for Dental Nurses in 1940. Appropriately, the school's building was designed to a high standard by the Government Architect's office under the direction of John Thomas Mair. It was constructed of reinforced concrete, with tōtara and mataī flooring, rimu and kauri joinery, steel windows, copper piping and granite front steps. Boilers in the basement provided central heating and electronic chair indicators summoned children to their fate. The building was converted into apartments in 2005 (Parlante Architectural Designers); the two added penthouse floors do not intrude on street views of the building.

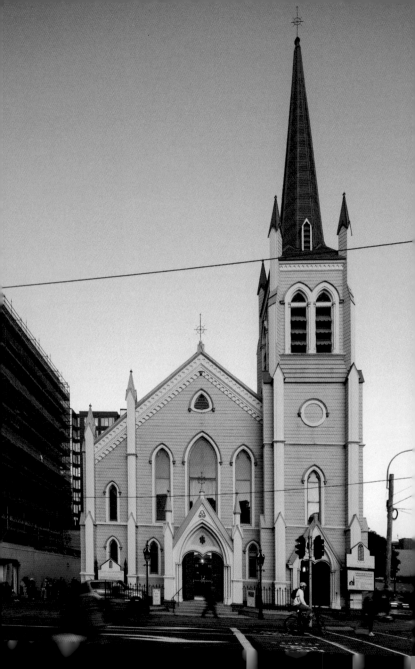

St Peter's

211 Willis Street

Thomas Turnbull, 1879
Historic Place Category 1

Thomas Turnbull was the pre-eminent Wellington architect of
the last quarter of the nineteenth century. Born in Glasgow and
orphaned at an early age, he trained as a carpenter before finding
work as a draughtsman in the Edinburgh office of David Bryce
(1803–1876), a successful Gothic Revival architect. Turnbull
immigrated to Australia in 1851, practising as an architect in
Victorian gold-rush towns before he and his wife, Louisa, moved
to San Francisco in 1861. He stayed there for a busy decade,
experiencing the destructive 1868 Hayward earthquake and
familiarising himself with contemporary earthquake-resistant
building technologies. Work, or rather the 'pressure of American
business tactics', affected his health and in 1871 he came to New
Zealand; Louisa and their five children arrived a year later. Turnbull
worked briefly for William Clayton, the Colonial Architect, before
setting up a practice that flourished over the next 30 years and was
continued by his son William (see pages 34–35).

Turnbull designed more than 300 buildings, most of them in
Wellington. Freemasonry, lawn bowls, the Wellington Caledonian
Society and his extensive library claimed his down time, and he also
served as a city councillor. Turnbull was fluent in the styles of his
age, but it was the Gothic Revival style that he principally applied
to St Peter's, the first of three timber churches he designed for
Protestant congregations in inner Wellington. Built of heart kauri,
St Peter's Gothicness is expressed in its lancet windows, pointed
arches, thin buttresses topped with pinnacles and a corner spire.
The interior combines plain white walls and timber panelling;
windows from the London stained glass manufacturer Lavers,
Barraud and Westlake were gifted post-construction. Turnbull
later made some modifications to the Anglican church as have,
over the past 130 years, architects Frederick de Jersey Clere, Bill
Alington and Hugh Tennent.

St John's

170 Willis Street

Thomas Turnbull, 1885
Historic Place Category 1

In May 1884, the Thomas Turnbull-designed Presbyterian St John's Church on Willis Street, which was only nine years old, was destroyed by fire. (The nineteenth-century New Zealand way of death for buildings; for humans, it was drowning.) One year later, 'a large number of ladies and gentlemen', reported *The Evening Post*, assembled to witness the laying of the foundation stone for a replacement church. Seven months later, 'upwards of 500 persons' attended the soirée celebrating the completion of the new St John's. This turnaround time for a significant building — the new St John's had seating for 800 worshippers — would be unthinkable now; even in 1885, it was recognised as extraordinary. Just getting the funding together so quickly was a momentous achievement, especially, as *The Evening Post* noted, in a piece of casual Victorian ethnic profiling, the St John's congregation consisted mainly of 'Scotchmen', and 'gentlemen of that nationality are not popularly credited with reckless prodigality'.

As it turned out, observed the minister of St John's, the destruction of the 1875 church had 'provided a blessing to the congregation'. The Presbyterians received, again from Turnbull, a 'much roomier and handsomer' building that added to the 'architectural beauty' of the city, and, incidentally, may well have surpassed the Anglican church up the road (see previous pages). On the elevated site, Turnbull designed a very pointy Gothic Revival church, facing north to the city, clad in rusticated weatherboards, with two square towers — one steeply ascending to the needle of its shingled spire, the other squatter, under its witch's hat — on either side of a Gothic-arched main entrance. On the east and west elevations buttresses bracket lancet windows. The interior, with its painted timber walls and kauri panelling, reveals Turnbull's stylistic eclecticism in such Classical elements as Corinthian capitals on the columns supporting the balcony.

Dixon Street Flats

134 Dixon Street

Government Architect,
Department of Housing Construction, 1944
Historic Place Category 1

The Dixon Street Flats are socially and politically important, and significant in their association with two of New Zealand's leading mid-twentieth-century architects. When the flats were finished in 1944 the welfare state already had a monumental presence in this part of town in the form of the nearby Dominion Training School for Dental Nurses (see pages 144–45). But this was the first appearance in the city of large-scale multi-unit Modernism. The Dixon Street Flats, which are still part of the state's rental stock, were a product of the social housing programme initiated by the Labour government upon winning office in 1935. Because the building so radically departed from the model of the standalone house it attracted political opposition, even within the Labour Party. The building's crime, in the eyes of social conservatives, was that its 115 apartments served not families, but single people and childless couples.

Dixon Street Flats were designed by the Department of Housing Construction (DHC) under Chief Architect Gordon Wilson, a very able designer who had worked for Gummer & Ford from the early 1920s to the mid-1930s. The building has a clearly expressed horizontality, especially on its rear elevation with its strata of balconies; window boxes relieve the austerity of the main façade. In its design, the DHC drew on European Modernist precedents. To what extent did it draw on the talents of a European Modernist architect? One of the DHC architects on the project was the Austrian émigré Ernst Plischke (1903–1992). In 1930s Vienna, Plischke had studied and worked with Modernist architects Peter Behrens and Josef Frank. Architectural historian Peter Shaw suggests Plischke didn't get the Dixon Street credit he deserved because Wilson was intimidated by him and his colleagues resented him. Another architectural historian, Julia Gatley, isn't so sure, saying Plischke's contribution is 'debated'.

Hotel St George

124 Willis Street

William John Prouse, 1930
Historic Place Category 2

The Hotel St George is one of Wellington's most significant Art Deco buildings, notable for its scale and the way it addresses the corner of its prominent site. The eight-storey building, constructed of earthquake-resistant, steel-reinforced concrete, was for decades the city's leading hotel. Guests included Henry Ford, Alfred Hitchcock, Jean Batten and Laurence Olivier. United States marines were billeted at the St George in the Second World War, the Beatles were besieged there during their 1964 New Zealand tour, and all sorts of rock groups and rugby teams have misbehaved in its corridors. The hotel is now run as a boarding house. The corner treatment is interesting; the obvious ways for a building to meet a corner are to hit it hard, in a no-nonsense right angle, or approach it more gently, with the point of the apex blunted or softened into a convex or even a concave curve. The Hotel St George takes the latter option and doubles down: the corner bay that separates the identical east and north elevations puffs out on its three lower levels, and inhales on the five upper levels. A rocket-like pattern of mouldings on the two main façades accentuates the building's verticality; decorative moulding above the corner balconies and first-floor windows provides a horizontal counterpoint.

The building's architect was William John Prouse, who came from a family of timber merchants in the Taranaki town of Pātea. He doesn't seem to have had formal architecture training, but was, as a former colleague described him, a 'go-getter'. (It wasn't meant as a compliment.) Prouse designed many buildings around Wellington. Around the time of the First World War, he and Jack Hoggard formed a partnership, later joined by William Henry Gummer. In 1932, Prouse entered a long-running architectural partnership with Norman Wilson (1901–1973).

St Mary of the Angels

17–27 Boulcott Street

Clere & Williams, 1922
Historic Place Category 1

The church serving the Catholic parish of central Wellington succeeded two earlier buildings on the site: a small church built in 1843 and a larger timber church built in 1874 and named after the very grand basilica in Assisi, Santa Maria degli Angeli. After that church was destroyed in a fire in 1918 the commission for its replacement went to Frederick de Jersey Clere, then in partnership with Llewellyn Edwin Williams. Clere, the son of a Lancashire clergyman, trained with English ecclesiastical architects before immigrating to New Zealand in 1877. He was still in his twenties when he was appointed as architect to the Anglican diocese of Wellington and went on to a long career in which he designed more than 100 churches, many constructed of reinforced concrete.

Clere designed the new St Mary of the Angels in the Gothic Revival style; the inspiration, reportedly, was the Cathedral of St Michael and St Gudula in Brussels, built, to a typical cathedral schedule, from the thirteenth to the sixteenth centuries. Clere's use of reinforced concrete — construction was undertaken by labourers supervised by the parish priest — allowed for a delicate expression of Gothic perpendicularity, evident in the slim towers that frame the façade and the slender columns and arches in the church's interior. The focus of the east-facing façade is a large rose window above the three Gothic arches of the church's entrance. The church features one of New Zealand's best clerestory treatments in the form of the stained glass windows illustrating the parables and miracles of Jesus, above the nave, and the crucifixion window above the sanctuary. Clere designed the marble reredos behind the altar. St Mary of the Angels, which recently was restored and earthquake-proofed (Bulleyment Fortune Architects and Ian Bowman, 2017), deserves to sit above a plaza, but holds its own among the adjacent buildings.

Antrim House

63 Boulcott Street

Thomas Turnbull & Son, 1904
Historic Place Category 1

Having trained as a bootmaker, Robert Hannah (1845–1930) left his home in County Antrim in the north of Ireland when he was around 18, migrating to Australia. A few years later he headed to New Zealand's West Coast and opened a shop in the gold-rush town of Charleston. In 1873, when the gold was gone, he moved to Wellington, opened a shoe shop and then a bootmaking factory, designed by Thomas Turnbull. Soon Robert Hannah & Co. had stores around New Zealand. The firm's founder was wealthy, a hard businessman, paternalistic employer and pillar of St John's Presbyterian Church (see pages 148–49). He and his wife, Hannah — by marrying him she committed herself to a tautonymous relationship — were parents of seven children.

In 1904 Hannah commissioned Thomas Turnbull & Son, by this time led by Thomas's son William, to design a home for his family on an elevated half-acre site on fashionable Boulcott Street. William Turnbull designed an 18-room house, built of kauri and tōtara, with pressed zinc ceilings and stained glass lead lights, in the Edwardian Italianate style. There's a suggestion of the antebellum mansions of the American South in the house's symmetrical disposition around a two-storey portico, its wide verandahs and profusion of paired Doric columns. The ornate façade includes quoins and keystones, the sort of faux stone detailing that aggravated Gothic Revival purists. The cupola topping the tower that rises above the mansard roofs was altered after a fire in 1940. After the Hannahs died, Antrim became a private hotel, then a bed-and-breakfast, and finally a hostel for young male public servants. In the late 1970s, its fall was arrested when the Historic Places Trust took over the building and restored it; the organisation, now called Heritage New Zealand Pouhere Taonga, continues to occupy Antrim House.

Plimmer House

99 Boulcott Street

Charles Tringham, 1874
Historic Place Category 1

In the nineteenth century you didn't need an architecture degree, or the approval of a licensing board, to be an architect. (Generally, however, you had to have been born male.) The paths to architectural practice, and architect status, followed the same courses they had for centuries: through articling, a form of apprenticeship which bound a pupil to an architect, or through the building trades. English migrant Charles Tringham (1841–1916) arrived in New Zealand in 1864 as a young carpenter and set himself up in Wellington as builder and undertaker. (Coffin-maker may have been a more accurate description.) Within a year he was advertising himself as an architect and soon after he married a daughter of New Zealand's Registrar-General. His career launched, he went on to design several hundred buildings before retiring to a farm in the Wairarapa in the 1890s.

In 1873 Tringham invited tenders for a 'Gentleman's Residence' in Boulcott Street, his client being civil servant Henry Eustace de Bathe Brandon (1840–1886), son of a prominent early settler. The timber house, which was later associated with the Plimmers, another notable settler family, is a rare surviving example of Carpenter Gothic. Two gables, one taller and steeper and both decorated with fretwork and finials, are arranged asymmetrically on either side of a small octagonal tower. The house survived threatened removal in the late 1960s and since the 1970s has served as a restaurant. In the early 1980s it was moved closer to the street, allowing an office building designed by Gordon Moller of the practice Craig Craig Moller to share the site at a deferential distance, while still communicating a lineage connection. With its verandahs, pointy gables and skinny tower, the newer building tiptoes along the line between homage and pastiche, graphically expressing the colonial vernacular inspiration of 1970s and 1980s Wellington Post-modernism.

Majestic Centre

88–100 Willis Street

Manning Mitchell and Jasmax, 1991

At 116 metres high, the 30-storey Majestic Centre is the tallest building in Wellington. Like all buildings, it is expressive of its time, and, because of its scale, dramatically so. Architecture this big demonstrates the economic and technical capacity of a society, and also plots a point on the urban graph that illustrates the relationship between private interest and the common good. What is the civic tolerance for developers' ambition, and what are the compromises and compliances that shape a building? The Majestic Centre was envisaged as a landmark. The building, which is clad in red granite and aluminium composite panels, starts with a three-storey atrium and ends with a halo of lights (a tribute to the nearby St Mary of the Angels, or a profane gesture of superiority?).

The Majestic Centre was the product of a hubristic moment. Conceived before the 1987 stock market crash, it was completed just before the 1991 recession took hold. The developers got a tower that obstructs views of the city from the hill behind it. They had to save an adjacent listed heritage building — 'Dr Pollen's House' (1902), a Second Empire concoction by William Turnbull — but were allowed to move it down Boulcott Street to its present corner site. On the other side of the Majestic Centre, they had to retain, but only as a façade, the listed Preston's Building (1912), designed in Edwardian Classical style by Francis Penty (1841–1919). The Majestic Centre's partially curved form is a response to wind-mitigating parameters established by the city council; the basement of the building, which is located in the middle of a walkable city with an extensive bus network, has 260 carparks. The building was designed by Jack Manning (1928–2021), who 30 years earlier was the architect of the AMP Building (1962), Auckland's first glass curtain-wall tower.

Telecom House

13–27 Manners Street

Athfield Architects, 1988

There was no shortage of surprises about Ian Athfield, but the corporate portfolio of New Zealand architecture's great larrikin was one of the more remarkable aspects of his story. It wasn't as if he was unfamiliar with commercial projects. After graduating from the University of Auckland's School of Architecture, he spent five years — three of them as a partner — with Structon Group, a sizeable Wellington practice which did a lot of large-scale work. Rather, when he went out on his own, free-wheeling Ath would seem to have been an unnatural candidate for corporate selection. However, he was ambitious, and unfazed by big projects and the people who commissioned them. (One memorable photograph of Ath captured him with Imelda Marcos at an exhibition of Athfield Architects' 1978 competition-winning, but unrealised, scheme for a 500-dwelling housing development in Manila.) He was pragmatic, too, happily confessing to architect and writer Gerald Melling, another Wellington iconoclast (see pages 92–93), that he saw commercial work 'as an opportunity to make money'. Something had to subsidise the continual additions to his extraordinary house, spreading down a hill above the Hutt Motorway, and also his firm's low-budget housing and community projects.

By the mid-1980s, drawing on the skill of long-time staff members such as Graeme Boucher and Ian Dickson, Athfield Architects was ready to answer the call of developers caught up in the tulip-mania of New Zealand's deregulation property boom. Telecom House is a 14-storey tower, clad in green ceramic tiles and green-tinted glass, and incorporating five terracotta-clad apartments. The building shows the signs, especially in its columned parapet, of Ath's mid-career Post-modernist inclinations. It also echoes, on its south (Manners Street) side, the wavy façade of Gummer & Ford's State Insurance Building (1942; see pages 188–89), to which Athfield Architects added a three-storey top in 1998.

Hibernian Building

89 Willis Street

Francis Drummond Stewart, 1930

The Hibernian Building puts on a brave Art Deco face as it traverses an awkward site angled acutely at Willis Street and obliquely at an alley heading off Bond Street. On its back sides only a lick of paint decorates the building's reinforced concrete structure, but its publicly visible façades — the narrow elevation on Willis Street, the wider side on Bond Street, and the corner where they meet — are clad in polychromatic brick and topped with a plaster parapet that adds a floor's worth of height to the five-storey building. Adding to the vertical effect is the chevron pattern — a favourite Art Deco motif and perhaps a reference to the building's wedge shape — of the parapet and the brickwork on the apex tower. (The tower's turret was removed after strong earthquakes in 1942.) The fenestration, especially the tall, thin windows on the main corner façade, also has a stretching effect.

The building was commissioned by, and occupied for half a century by, H. Nimmo & Sons' music shop and warehouse, and assumed its present title when it was bought by the Hibernian Society, a Catholic mutual aid organisation. It was designed by Francis Drummond Stewart (1902–1972), who had a 30-year career in the public sector, including wartime service as Officer of Works and Camouflage for the New Zealand army and a long stint (1952–1968) as Assistant Government Architect. From 1926 to 1936, though, Stewart was the in-house architect for the Hibernian Building's contractor, Fletcher Construction. The building company founded in Dunedin by commercially and politically astute Scottish immigrant James Fletcher (1886–1974) was rising to national pre-eminence in the early 1930s. Soon it would be building the National Art Gallery and Dominion Museum (see pages 136–37), Wellington Railway Station (see pages 224–27) and hundreds of state houses around New Zealand.

Telecom Central

40–52 Willis Street and Boulcott Street

architecture+, 2011

In designing the Telecom Central building, now known as Spark Central, Wellington practice architecture+ turned what could have been a mundane commercial project into a diverting piece of city-scaled sculpture. The 12-storey office complex — plus a couple of carpark levels — comprises two towers, one fronting Willis Street to the east and the other Boulcott Street to the west, opposite Antrim House (see pages 156–57). The towers meet in a central atrium that rises above the pedestrian throughway connecting the two building entrances. The distinguishing feature on both sides of the building is the glass curtain wall, which has been divided vertically into several elements — five on the Willis Street-facing façade and four on the Boulcott Street elevation — bordered by concrete edges and gold-coloured anodised aluminium sun screens. More dramatically, these façade elements are also divided horizontally, and asymmetrically, into glazed sections that slope inwards or outwards at an angle of 40 centimetres per floor. The effect of the façade treatment is most evident when viewed from further down Willis Street, looking to the south; the glass wall is particularly striking when viewed from Chews Lane, directly opposite the Willis Street entrance.

At ground level, the immediate focus of the Willis Street pedestrian is the portion of the heritage structure that has been incorporated into the building. This exercise in façadism has preserved the foyer and fancy face — rusticated masonry, projecting bays, floral swags, keystones and consoles — of the three-storey Macarthy Building, better known as the Tisdalls Building after the sports shop that occupied it for half a century. That building was commissioned by Mary Macarthy, widow of property investor and philanthropist Thomas George Macarthy, and constructed in 1913 to the design of Joseph McClatchey Dawson (c1876–1956), later a partner in the practice King & Dawson.

1 Willis Street

Stephenson & Turner, 1984

Few New Zealand building projects have been as controversial as the construction of what was originally called the BNZ Centre. And few buildings so clearly demonstrate the difference between popular and professional perspectives on architecture. While many of the public view the all-black 30-storey tower as an ominous monument to corporate arrogance, architectural defenders of the building cite its austere clarity and minimalist elegance. The 102-metre tower was the tallest building in the country when completed and was always going to get a lot of attention, but it became much more than an architecture story. Its construction generated an epic industrial conflict and turned into a financial debacle. (The budget blew out by 400 per cent.)

The building was conceived in the late 1960s as the head-quarters for the then state-owned Bank of New Zealand. Bank executives and architects from Stephenson & Turner toured the world, visiting high-rise buildings. Evidently, they were impressed — and why not? — by Ludwig Mies van der Rohe's Seagram Building (New York, 1957) and also by Melbourne's BHP House (1972), designed with help from American International Style specialists Skidmore, Owings & Merrill. (Stephenson & Turner had already expressed their admiration for SOM at Shell House; see pages 246–47). What subsequently emerged from Stephenson & Turner's drawing boards was a tower with a steel frame, capable of flexing by up to 300 millimetres to withstand Wellington's winds, and a sheer façade of Brazilian black granite and dark glass. Construction began in 1974 and ended a decade later, after a years-long stand-off between the militant Boilermakers Union — the union for steelworkers — and the anti-union National government led by Prime Minister Robert Muldoon. The design implication of this long gestation was a building that looked dated when finally completed; the construction consequence was a pivot from steel to reinforced concrete as the structural material in big buildings.

ROUTE 4:
CBD

CIRCA 2.5 KILOMETRES

This circular route around the big-business heart
of the city takes in significant institutional and
commercial buildings, many of them from the inter-
war years in which Wellington's downtown was
shaped. This is the part of Wellington where the city
feels most urban, thanks to Lambton Quay's wall of
buildings and the dense occupation of Featherston
Street and Customhouse Quay. Greed, convenience
and civic carelessness took their architectural toll in
the late twentieth century, but many fine buildings
remain, as does the area's coherent streetscape.
The precinct's substance was underwritten by
the banks and insurance companies that built to
impress in the first half of the twentieth century.
The evolution of the city's architecture is evident
in buildings that reveal a range of influences
and express a century of stylistic succession as
varieties of revivalism — Classical, Georgian,
Baroque — gave way to Art Deco, Stripped Moderne
and full-blown, glass curtain-wall Modernism.

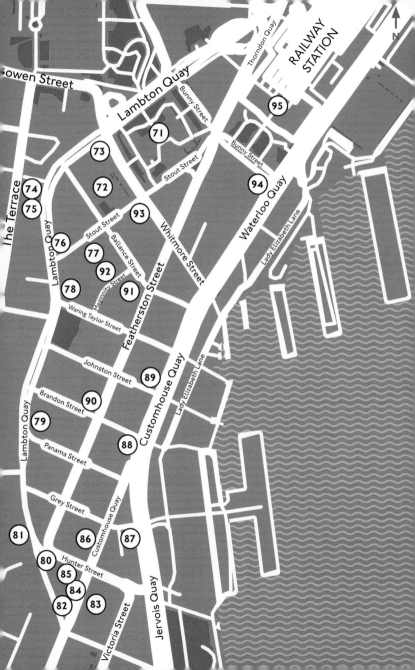

Old Government Building

55 Lambton Quay

William Clayton, Colonial Architect, 1876
Historic Place Category 1

Old Government Building is big — around 9500 square metres in floor area — but even so, it's surprising to think it once housed all of Wellington's civil servants. Actually, its provision was testament to the rapid growth of the bureaucracy. In 1867, the colony had 1600 civil servants; a decade later there were 11,000. (Almost all were male; when Grace Neill was appointed as New Zealand's first female factory inspector in 1894, she was the only woman working in the Government Building.) The rise of the public service was a consequence of the expansionist economic policy of Julius Vogel (1835–1899), who became Colonial Treasurer in 1869 and served as Premier from 1873–1876, and the abolition of provincial government in 1875.

Colonial Architect William Clayton designed the Government Building around 1873. Tenders were called for, in concrete, which Clayton preferred, and timber; the cost of concrete decided the choice of timber. (The building snuck under the wire of the city council's 1877 prohibition of fire-prone timber buildings in the CBD.) Construction began in 1875 and was challenging. The site was on reclaimed land surrounded on three sides by water. (This did allow timber to be landed by scow.) A sawmill was erected on the site, tōtara piles were driven into the seabed, tradesmen were sourced from Britain, and the budget was blown. However, the building was finished in 22 months, a remarkable feat from the perspective of our slower, more complicated construction era. As built, the government's new executive premises — even now claimed to be the world's largest timber building — included 143 rooms, 126 fireplaces, 22 chimneys, eight verandahs, seven porticos and 64 toilets. (Women's bathrooms were added 20 years later.)

The building William Clayton designed is H-shaped and symmetrically arranged around the porte-cochère in the middle of its main north–south axis. It is a Renaissance-style building; that is, a building in the masonry tradition. The fact that Clayton couldn't use masonry materials didn't lead him to rethink the design. He just treated wood as stone. Thus, kauri weatherboards are rusticated and wooden blocks imitate stone quoins. Each floor gets a string course, in timber. There's a triangular pediment above the main entrance and windows with, on alternate floors, arches, triangular pediments and square lintels. There are keystones, corbels and consoles. And, of course, Doric columns at the main entry. As historian David Kernohan notes, the Government Building is Western architectural history come full circle. The temples of Classical Greece were timber forms rendered in stone. More than two millennia later, on Lambton Quay, the borrowing was reversed. The façade of the Government Building, and its foundations and interior, including the wonderful cantilevered staircases, were rehabilitated when the Department of Conservation restored the building in the 1990s. In 1996 the building was handed over to Victoria University's Faculty of Law.

William Clayton was New Zealand's first, and only, Colonial Architect. (John Campbell was appointed first Government Architect in 1909.) He was born in 1823 in Tasmania — when it was still Van Diemen's Land — and schooled there before going to London for architectural training. In 1848, and newly married to Emily Samson, he returned to Tasmania, where, over the next 15 years, he designed more than 300 buildings. In 1863, the Claytons and their six children moved to gold-rush Dunedin. Clayton partnered with William Mason (1810–1897) — later a co-founder of Mason & Wales, New Zealand's oldest surviving architecture practice — for six years, before the gold ran out. In 1869 he offered his services to the government as Colonial Architect and moved with his family to Wellington. (His daughter Mary was already living there, as the wife of Julius Vogel.) Again, there was much for Clayton to do. Vogel's public works programme included myriad buildings — 80 post offices, between 1870 and 1877, plus courthouses, prisons, schools and hospitals. Clayton also undertook private work. His purposeful life ended sadly. With his wife and children away in England in 1877, Clayton visited Dunedin, where an old ankle injury, caused by a buggy accident, became inflamed. Amputation was prescribed and, reported *The Southland Times*, Clayton 'gradually sank under the operation'. Emily Clayton spent the rest of her life in England.

Supreme Court Building (Former)

36–42 Stout Street and Whitmore and Ballance Streets

Pierre Finch Martineau Burrows,
Public Works Department, 1881
Historic Place Category 1

On 1 December 1879 the foundation stone for the new Courts of Justice, known through most of its history as the Supreme Court Building, was laid in what *The Evening Post* called 'the most imposing public ceremonial which probably has ever yet been witnessed in New Zealand'. Proving that the past is a foreign country, the public event was organised by the Freemasons. Militia units paraded, Masons marched and a choir sang. In the procession, following behind the stewards of the ritual tools of plumb, level and square, and bearing building plans, was 'Brother Burrows' of Lodge 463 — Pierre Finch Martineau Burrows (1842–1920); that is, Chief Draughtsman in the Department of Public Works, and architect of the Courts of Justice.

Burrows, an English migrant of Huguenot descent, worked under Colonial Architect William Clayton (see previous pages). When Clayton died, Burrows succeeded to his role but, curiously, not his title or salary. (Perhaps Burrows lacked connections; perhaps the government was having one of its fits of parsimony.) On a site with three street frontages, Burrows designed a neo-Classical building two storeys high on the arms of its T-shape, with flanking single-storey pavilions. The ground level is rusticated with round-arched windows; the upper floor features pilasters and columns with Composite capitals, square-headed windows and triangular pediments. Unlike the Government Building, the Supreme Court was captured by the city council's 1877 proscription of combustible cladding. Supported on tōtara piles driven through reclaimed land, the Supreme Court thus became Wellington's first substantial masonry building, the 1855 magnitude 8.2 earthquake having hitherto scared off such construction. The building was abandoned in the 1990s; after a heritage campaign it was restored (2010) by Warren and Mahoney and conservation architect Chris Cochran.

Supreme Court of New Zealand

85 Lambton Quay and Whitmore and Ballance Streets

Warren and Mahoney, 2010

In any democracy a big public architecture project is heavily freighted. Everyone's paying, so everyone's entitled to an opinion. The pressure on architects increases further when a project occurs in the context of institutional or even societal change. The National Library (see pages 262–63) was a case in point, as was Te Papa (see pages 38–41). For the architects of the Supreme Court of New Zealand, the challenge was perhaps even more daunting: to produce a design expression of profoundly altered constitutional arrangements. The building was commissioned to house the Supreme Court after it came into being in 2004 as New Zealand's highest court, replacing the British Privy Council as the country's court of last resort. (The old Supreme Court, and its building, see previous pages, had been renamed the High Court in 1980.)

By the time Warren and Mahoney received the commission for the new court, it had been decided to restore its venerable neighbour. The old and new buildings would be site-mates. Should the new building defer to the old, or should it represent, architecturally, New Zealand's clean break from juridical dependency? And in either case, what else should the building symbolise? Design architect Roy Wilson said the decision was to go 'small and special, rather than tall and commercial'. (An interesting polarity of options.) The resulting building, oriented on an axis shared with the old Supreme Court Building, is low and square; it has a plinth and columns and a hole in the middle — rather Villa Savoye, a critic wrote — admitting light to the elliptical 'kauri cone' courtroom. Transparency and indigeneity are expressed in a bronze screen that alludes to the branches of rātā and pōhutukawa trees. In 2010, after all this effort to signal New Zealand's judicial sovereignty, the Supreme Court was opened by Prince William.

Manchester Unity Building

120 Lambton Quay and 43 The Terrace

Structon Group, 1966

Just as there are some things that can't be unsaid, so there are some images that once conjured can't be forgotten. It's hard to look at the façade of the Manchester Unity Building — the original name of the building at 120 Lambton Quay, which is now serviced apartments — without recalling Ian Athfield's reported description of it as a 'vertical cemetery'. If Ath said that, he had a point. The building's honeycomb of stretched hexagons does resemble a stack of coffins. The Manchester Unity Building has another reputational cross to bear: its invidious adjacency to Massey House (see overleaf), a perennial architectural favourite. And yet: at least Structon Group, and in particular design architect Keith Cooper (1926–2011), was trying to do something a bit different. And at least the Manchester Unity Building was obliged to match the height of the earlier Massey House by adhering to what was the council-mandated 30.6-metre datum line of Lambton Quay's continuous west wall of joined-up buildings. (The relationship was repeated on the buildings' other street sides, facing The Terrace.)

Cooper, the son of English migrants who joined the firm of King & Dawson when he was 16, was a naturally talented designer with an imaginative and even quixotic side (for example, the Racing Conference Building, see pages 114–15). Not that he was about to bust out of the New Zealand intellectual straitjacket stitched from settler pragmatism and British empiricism. An interview with Cooper in 2005 convinced architectural historian Christine McCarthy that he 'wasn't the kind of architect interested in complex architectural theory — he aligned with the Chamber of Commerce, not the NZIA [New Zealand Institute of Architects]'. Proud of his commercial sensibility, Cooper emphasised to his interviewer that while the Manchester Unity Building and Massey House are the same height, he had squeezed in another floor of lettable space.

Massey House

126–134 Lambton Quay and 45–55 The Terrace

Plischke & Firth, 1952
Historic Place Category 1

Ernst Plischke (1903–1992) graduated from Vienna's Academy of
Fine Arts in 1926, worked for Modernist architects Peter Behrens
(1868–1940) and Josef Frank (1885–1967), and was a member
of the Bauhaus-like Austrian Werkbund. In 1939, after the Nazis
annexed Austria, he immigrated to New Zealand with his Jewish
wife Anna (1895–1983) and stayed for 25 years. Plischke was
accomplished and intense, and New Zealand — Anglocentric and
Anglo-mannered — never seemed to know what to make of him.
The suspicion was to an extent reciprocated. Plischke worked for the
Department of Housing Construction (DHC; see pages 150–51)
and wrote and gave public lectures about architecture and design. In
1947, he was rejected for the Design Chair at Auckland University's
School of Architecture in favour of an English Beaux-Arts academic,
and in the same year left the DHC for private practice in Wellington.
(Anna would design the gardens for many of his projects.)

In 1948, Plischke received his most important New Zealand
commission — Massey House, an eight-storey government building
on Lambton Quay, which he designed in partnership with Clifton
Firth (1908–1994), also a former DHC staffer. Massey House
was New Zealand's first curtain-walled office building; that is, its
aluminium-framed glass walls facing both Lambton Quay and The
Terrace function as skin, not structure. The building has Corbusian
pilotis on the ground floor and a Corbusian balcony at the top
floor: the International Style, in 1957, had arrived in Wellington
(having taken nine years from initial design to do so). Massey
House, which for decades famously housed Parson's Bookshop
and the coffee house started by Jewish émigré Harry Seresin —
both designed by Plischke — received a complementary southern
extension in 1967. This was designed by Clifton Firth, the Plischkes
having returned to Vienna in 1963, when Ernst accepted the
position of professor of architecture at the Academy of Fine Arts.

Public Trust Building

131–135 Lambton Quay and Stout Street

John Campbell, Architect, Public Works Department, 1909
Historic Place Category I

On 9 June 1909, in bold disregard for the event's optics, 150 guests sat down to what Wellington's *Free Lance* newspaper described as 'an exceptionally jolly' banquet to mark the opening of the government's Public Trust Building. Commencing with oysters, the menu 'ranged through lobster and chicken mayonnaise, by way of roast turkey with truffles, and roast duckling, and past a series of roast joints with French and Italian sauces'. Champagne was 'popping and fizzing on all hands'. Also audacious was the presence of many female guests. 'How much better this is than having solid rows of mere men tucking into the good things of this life, and leaving the ladies out in the cold altogether!', commented *The Free Lance*. The attendance of 'the ladies' was particularly appropriate. Women especially benefited from the existence of the Public Trust, which had been established in 1872 by Julius Vogel (see pages 172–75) to protect estates or inheritances from dishonest administration. Eventually, the government voted money for a Public Trust Building and allotted it a site on reclaimed land. Seismic concerns prompted the engagement in 1904 of Reid & Reid, a Californian firm specialising in the design of earthquake-resistant buildings. Controversy ensued, and the government then turned to its own designer, John Campbell (1857–1942), architect in the Public Works Department and soon to be — from 1909–1922 — Government Architect.

Scottish-born and -trained Campbell, with his colleague Llewellyn Lincoln Richards (1865–1945), produced an Edwardian Baroque concoction, a five-storey building with a riveted steel frame clad in Nelson granite and bricks made at Mount Cook Gaol. The major of many eclectic features are three large segmental arches, supported by Corinthian columns (best viewed from Stout Street), and the corner drum with its copper crown. The building was saved from demolition in the 1980s and restored by Warren and Mahoney. It now houses the Ministry for Culture and Heritage.

Departmental Building

15 Stout Street and Ballance and Maginnity Streets

John Thomas Mair, Government Architect,
Public Works Department, 1940
Historic Place Category 2

Sixty-five years after the first growth spurt of the New Zealand bureaucracy prompted the construction of the Government Building (see pages 172–75), the civil service got another big Wellington building to fill. The Departmental Building was designed by Government Architect John Thomas Mair in 1935. Just as well — the election that year of the first Labour government gave a further boost to Wellington as a public service town. Construction was delayed by the need to acquire more land, and later by material substitutions necessitated by wartime shortages. For all the difficulties in producing a large civic building in a period bracketed by the Depression and the war, the Public Works Department and Fletcher Construction delivered an impressive result. Over the course of a career that included a Beaux-Arts architectural education at the University of Pennsylvania, Mair edged his way towards Modernism, getting as far as the Art Deco/Streamline Moderne style he used on the Cambridge Terrace Post Office (see pages 80–81) and the Dominion Training School for Dental Nurses (see pages 144–45), as well as the Departmental Building. Mair was Government Architect from 1923–1941, and architectural historian Peter Richardson sees his cautious approach to Modernism as being harmonious with Prime Minister Michael Joseph Savage's gentle approach to socialism.

The Departmental Building is Modernism without hard edges. The eight-storey building — a penthouse was added in the 1950s — bulkily occupies half a city block. Its heft is offset by the horizontal sweep of its spandrels and the rounded 'book ends', with curved windows, that frame the recessed entrance on Stout Street. The building was constructed in reinforced concrete and clad in Putāruru stone above a granite base. Water seepage eroded the stonework, some of which was ground up into the quartz panels with which the building was reclad in the 1980s.

State Insurance Building
(Former)

143–149 Lambton Quay, and Stout and Waring Taylor Streets

Gummer & Ford, 1942
Historic Place Category 1

The State Insurance Building is one of the most assured architectural works in Wellington's CBD. It was commissioned by the government-owned State Insurance Company, which was established in 1903 to disrupt the dominance of foreign financial institutions. In response to the company's success, the Arcadia Hotel (James Bennie, 1905) on Lambton Quay was demolished in 1939 to provide the site for a building, designed by Gummer & Ford. It was a high-quality building, eight storeys high and constructed of reinforced concrete clad in Coromandel tonalite (magmatic stone) and a render of quartz-sand plaster. The interior foyer and stairwell were lined with marble. Masterfully, the building turns the challenge of an obtusely angled site to design advantage. On both the Stout Street and Waring Taylor Street elevations, the façade ripples in waves away from the chamfered corner with its double-height portal and pair of lion-topped columns.

The building is one of the most impressive designs of the practice led by William Henry Gummer (1884–1966) and Charles Reginald Ford (1880–1972). Gummer was a veteran of the Mounted Rifles Brigade and, pre-First World War, the offices of Edwin Lutyens in London and Daniel Burnham in Chicago. Ford was an anti-conscription campaigner, member of Robert Falcon Scott's first Antarctic expedition (1901–1904), and author of a pioneering study of construction seismic hazards. The State Insurance Building has a familial likeness to the Shell Building in Berlin (1932; Emil Farhrenkamp). Historian Bruce Petry thought the design of the building evidenced collaboration between Gummer & Ford's historicist founding partners and younger architects in the firm. The State Insurance Building was saved from demolition in the 1980s; in the late 1990s, a controversial, three-storey rooftop addition was designed by Athfield Architects.

DIC Department Store (Former)

179–193 Lambton Quay

Anketell & K. Henderson with Atkins & Mitchell, 1929
Historic Place Category 2

For most of last century, two of Wellington's department stores were competitive neighbours on Lambton Quay. From the 1890s, the posher Kirkcaldie & Stains progressively spread itself across the block between Brandon and Johnston Streets in a series of buildings and additions designed by Thomas Turnbull & Son, and given a unified Lambton Quay façade by Llewellyn Edwin Williams in the late 1920s. The Drapery and General Importing Company (DIC) arrived a bit later on Lambton Quay. The company had been started in 1884 by clothing merchant Bendix Hallenstein (1835–1905), who was born in the Duchy of Brunswick and arrived in New Zealand in 1863 via Manchester and the Victorian gold fields. (The Hallenstein chain of stores around New Zealand survives as a brand to this day.) By the mid-1920s the DIC had wrested control of the block between Brandon and Panama Streets, and it then commissioned a department store. The noted Melbourne firm founded by Anketell Henderson (1852–1922) and continued by his son Kingsley (1883–1942) collaborated on the project with Wellington practice Atkins & Mitchell (see pages 200–01, 222–23).

The Kirkcaldie & Stains building got two 13-storey towers (Morrison, Cooper & Partners) dumped on top of it in the late 1980s, but history has been kinder to the DIC building. Even though the DIC business fell into the hands of asset stripper Ron Brierley, again in the 1980s, its seven-storey, steel-framed Lambton Quay building has survived as a good example of Chicago School architecture. It expresses that style's Classically derived articulation of beginning (base), middle (shaft) and end (capital). Above the two-storey verandahed pediment, five-storey pilasters rise to meet the eighth floor, which is treated as an entablature capped with a bracketed cornice. A pair of giant Corinthian columns frame the building's main entrance on Lambton Quay.

MLC Building (Former)

231 Lambton Quay

Mitchell & Mitchell, 1940
Historic Place Category 1

What an architecture practices does is design buildings, but what it is is a business. Over time, if a practice prospers, new partners come on board as old ones depart. The practice may change its name, but cautiously, as it balances the benefits of continuity and contemporaneity. The history of Mitchell & Mitchell illustrates the dynastic nature of architecture practices as commercial entities. Thus, the 1880s Whanganui firm of Atkins & Clere morphed into the Wellington firm of Atkins & Bacon, which employed Cyril Hawthorn Mitchell (1891–1949) in 1918. By 1919, Alfred Atkins was dead, Roger Bacon had left Wellington, and Mitchell was left in charge of the practice which he renamed as Atkins & Mitchell. His younger brother Allan Hawthorn Mitchell joined him in 1932, and in 1937 he finally felt free to operate in the nominative present as Mitchell & Mitchell. Cyril Mitchell was well connected to Wellington business and finance interests (see pages 74–75, 190–91, 200–01, 222–23), and in the late 1930s the Mitchells' busy practice was commissioned to design the New Zealand head office of the Australian-owned Mutual Life and Citizens' Assurance Company (MLC).

On the nine-storey Lambton Quay building Mitchell & Mitchell deployed the Art Deco/Moderne style then preferred by the MLC. The building shares the elegant verticality and warm, buff-coloured appearance of the MLC Building on Martin Place, Sydney (Bates, Smart & McCutcheon, 1938). Like its larger Sydney sibling, Wellington's MLC Building has a rhythmic façade of tall piers framing pairs of windows separated by slender mullions. Above a base of red Kanimbla granite from north Queensland, the building is clad in terracotta tiles. At its apex corner it rises to a clock tower topped with the MLC's symbol in relief: a Classical figure trying unsuccessfully to break a bundle of rods — in retrospect, a rather Fascist image — that alluded to the MLC motto: union is strength.

ROUTE 4–80

326–340 Lambton Quay

South British Insurance Company Building (326), Keith Draffin, 1936; CBA Building (328–330), Clere & Clere, 1936; Prudential Assurance Building (332–340), Gray Young, Morton & Young, 1935

Historic Place Category 2

This trio of buildings constructed as New Zealand was emerging from the Great Depression provides a snapshot of the architectural styles of their time and evidence of the role of banks and insurance companies in shaping the streetscape of twentieth-century Wellington. At 326 Lambton Quay the neo-Georgian and Chicago styles meet in an austere, six-storey mini-tower clad in imported Darleydale sandstone. Keith Draffin (1890–1964) gave the head office of the New Zealand-owned South British Insurance Company a rusticated base and a frugal allowance of façade decoration at its piano nobile level — small pilasters, a Greek meander-pattern border and a pair of relief panels, one, it seems, depicting Hermes, the other perhaps Ares. Next door, at 328–330 Lambton Quay, Clere & Clere, with assistance from Melbourne practice Anketell & K. Henderson (see pages 190–91), designed the New Zealand head office of the Commercial Bank of Australia (CBA). The eight-storey, steel-framed building follows the Chicago style of base, shaft and capital. Four fluted columns two storeys high — now over-clad at ground level — support a frieze, above which piers frame spandrel panels decorated with an Art Deco relief pattern.

The Prudential Assurance Building at 332–340 Lambton Quay is the most impressive of the sibling structures. Gray Young, Morton & Young and Sydney practice Hennessy & Hennessy designed the eight-storey Art Deco building to be viewed in the round. Above a base clad in artificial pink 'Benedict' stone, all four façades are vertical compositions of narrow piers with moulded spandrels. There are chevrons, stylised eagles as gargoyles and a crenellated parapet. The buildings at 326–340 Lambton Quay were saved from demolition in the 1990s; a four-storey apartment addition (2006) was later imposed on the Prudential Assurance Building.

BNZ Buildings 1 and 2
(Old Bank Arcade)

233–247 Lambton Quay and Customhouse Quay (Old Bank Arcade)

Thomas Turnbull & Son, 1901 and 1904
Historic Place Categories 1 (Building 1) and 2 (Building 2)

The triangular site bordered by Lambton Quay, Customhouse Quay and Hunter Street sits at a frontier of reclaimed Wellington and the original shoreline, preserved in contour by the winding course of Lambton Quay. This is the place where, in the twentieth century, the small-business end of the city came up against the big end of town. Between here and the government precinct, the streets were lined with the head offices of companies that dominated the private side of the New Zealand economy — banks, finance and insurance companies, legal firms, shipping concerns, producer boards. A dozen blocks laid out in a grid of streets constituted the most intensely urban environment in the country. At the tip of the triangle, at the top of Lambton Quay, presenting as the gateway to this moneyed enclave, was the Bank of New Zealand Building.

The Bank of New Zealand (BNZ), which was established in Auckland in 1861, bought a plot of land on one of the first Wellington reclamations and established a branch there in 1863. In 1890, in an early demonstration of New Zealand corporate hubris, the BNZ moved its head office to London. It then almost collapsed and was bailed out by the government, which insisted the bank base itself in Wellington. Accordingly, at the end of the decade the design commission for a new BNZ headquarters — later called BNZ Building No. 1 — on the site of the bank's Wellington branch was awarded to Thomas Turnbull & Son. By this stage, Thomas Turnbull was in partnership with his son William. When the architects released their design in 1898, *The New Zealand Mail* reckoned the 'magnificent new bankinghouse' in 'the classic style of the Italian Renaissance' would be 'one of the best' buildings in the country, 'if not absolutely the best'. Duly appalled at the BNZ's recidivist extravagance, the government demanded a redesign, and a downsizing from four to three storeys (plus basement).

Despite the mandatory design do-over, the Bank of New Zealand Building was extraordinarily ornate, and after a century and a quarter's worth of alterations it is still impressive. Thomas Turnbull was, in the late-Victorian manner, stylistically heterodox: he could do Gothic (see pages 90–91, 146–49), but just as happily shift into Classical or Renaissance mode, as he proved with the Bank of New Zealand Building. Constructed of load-bearing bricks on concrete foundations and rendered with plaster, the building is symmetrically arranged on its V-shaped site, with its prow at the junction of Lambton Quay and Customhouse Quay. It is organised horizontally in three levels. A cornice separates the heavily rusticated ground floor from two upper floors with distinctive window treatments: the first floor has square-headed windows framed with Corinthian columns, pseudo-balconies and triangular pediments; the second floor has arched windows framed by Doric pilasters topped by brackets, horizontal pediments and the entablature that surmounts the building. The neo-Classical pile-on peaks at the building's prow with its pair of entry arches, lion's-head corbels, balconies and double-height Corinthian pilasters.

Shortly after completing the Bank of New Zealand Building, Thomas Turnbull & Son designed a building right next door on Lambton Quay. The building was later bought by the BNZ and became known as BNZ Building No. 2. William Turnbull must have been the principal architect of the building; his father, Thomas, was by then nearly 80. 'BNZ Building No. 2' matches its neighbour in style and height, but its inclusion of an attic storey means the cornices and windows don't align. The symmetrical façade centres on a pair of arched doors topped by triangular pediments; above a rusticated base, double-height Corinthian pilasters unify the second and third floors, which have different window treatments.

Ownership of BNZ Buildings 1 and 2 was assumed by the city council in the 1980s. A decade of neglect preceded the sale of the buildings to the developer that had restored the Queen Victoria Building in Sydney. On that model, the BNZ Buildings were turned into an arcade.

Commercial Travellers and Warehousemen's Association Building (United Building)

107–109 Customhouse Quay

Atkins & Mitchell, with William Gray Young, 1929

The Wellington Commercial Travellers and Warehousemen's Association was founded in 1890 as a benevolent society 'to grant relief to the widows and orphans of commercial travellers who are left in indigent circumstances'. Soon, the stationary handlers of goods (warehousemen) were invited to join their itinerant sellers (commercial travellers) and by 1928 the Association had more than 1000 members. Time for a new building, the Commercial Travellers and Warehousemen's third. (The first dated from 1896; the second from 1905.) The Association held a design competition for a building on Customhouse Quay, which was won by Cyril Hawthorn Mitchell. At this time, Mitchell was sole director of Atkins & Mitchell, practice co-founder Alfred Atkins having died in 1919. (Atkins's claim to fame in the future will rest on the pioneering presence in his pre-war office of New Zealand's first female registered architect, Lucy Greenish, 1888–1976.) Mitchell's victory must have been bittersweet. While the clients liked his plan, they apparently preferred the neo-Georgian façade drawn by William Gray Young, so the two were combined.

If you wanted to present your building as an urban-scaled strip of neo-Georgian wallpaper, Gray Young was absolutely your man. Here, he gave Georgian detailing to an eight-storey building composed, Chicago-style, as base (now compromised by a verandah), shaft and capital. Above the plaster piano nobile floor with its arched windows are five floors of plain, square-headed windows flush with the brick façade. The top floor is given an arcade treatment. The building was sold in 1978; soon after, the Wellington Commercial Travellers and Warehousemen's Association was wound up.

National Mutual Life Building
(BNZ Building 3)

98–102 Customhouse Quay and Hunter Street (Old Bank Arcade)

Thomas Turnbull, 1885
Historic Place Category 1

On 14 October 1885, reported *The New Zealand Mail*, 80 'gentlemen' assembled in Wellington for one of the long lunches beloved of the Victorian and Edwardian bourgeoisie (see also pages 184–85). This time the event being marked was the opening of the new building of the National Mutual Life Association of Australasia. The 'mutual' — i.e., policyholder owned — insurer had been founded in Melbourne in 1869 and had operated in New Zealand since 1880. The local business, evidently, was already a success, sufficient to attract to the Wellington building launch the National Mutual's Board Chair, prominent Melbourne politician Edmund Langton (1828–1905). In his patronising oration, Langton confessed that, after a day in New Zealand, he was 'much struck' by 'the freshness of the people and the complexions of the young ladies'. He then turned to the building: 'Some of the ornamentation over the doors might be done without but when the cost was distributed over 50,000 or 60,000 policies it would not be much felt.'

Well, it's true enough: Thomas Turnbull had certainly designed a rich concoction. In inspiration, the masonry building is a Renaissance palazzo, symmetrical on both of its street façades, with a rusticated base and cornices separating two upper levels with different Classical window treatments. Arches, pediments, pilasters, consoles, corbels, brackets and entablature — all were pressed into service. The ornamentation that prompted Langton's barb was produced by plasterer Edmund Platt (1850–1927), whose façade contributions include urns, lions' heads, grotesques and festoons in the dental grip of caricatured figures. The building was sold to the Bank of New Zealand in 1963, becoming BNZ Building 3. It now connects to the Old Bank Arcade.

New Zealand Accident Insurance Company Building
(BNZ Building 4)

29 Hunter Street

Hislop & Walden, 1903

In colonial New Zealand accidents were just waiting to happen. Contemporary newspapers served up a steady diet of memento mori — accounts of floods and fires, shipwrecks and mine collapses, bolting horses and runaway buggies. It's no wonder companies providing insurance (for unforeseen occurrences) and assurance (for predictable events, i.e., death) proliferated. Historian Alan Henderson calculates that in 1893, when the country's population was around 700,000, New Zealand had 27 insurance and assurance companies. Many of them built imposing Wellington headquarters on the blocks between Lambton and Customhouse Quays. At the turn of the twentieth century, Hislop & Walden designed a head office for the New Zealand Accident Insurance Company. (The building was sold in 1938 to the Bank of New Zealand, became known as BNZ Building 4 and is now part of the Old Bank Arcade.) The masonry building is a pared-back version of its neo-Classical siblings in the BNZ family, with four levels arranged symmetrically into three vertical bays, divided horizontally by prominent cornices. The street façade centres on the large arched window on the raised ground floor and is unified by the stylised pilasters that ascend to an entablature capped by two triangular pediments with acroteria.

Hislop & Walden was a Dunedin-originated practice led by James Hislop (1859–1904) and his former pupil Edward Walter Walden (1870–1944). The year after the completion of the New Zealand Accident Insurance Company Building, Hislop — lawn bowler, Freemason and horse-racing fan — was found early one morning, unconscious and rain-soaked, by the side of a road, miles from home. A coronial inquest — attended by insurance interests — decided the cause of death was a perforated stomach.

AMP Building (Former)

86 Customhouse Quay and Hunter Street

Clere & Clere, 1928
Historic Place Category 1

The AMP Building on the corner of Customhouse Quay and Hunter Street is the most impressive building in what the city council calls the BNZ/Head Office Heritage Area. The building is advantaged by its scale — it was the first building constructed to the new city height limit of 102 feet, or 31 metres — and its disciplined ornamentation. Although inspired by the Italian Renaissance palazzo, and possessing the appropriate Classical ordering and elements, the building doesn't have the thick marzipan façade of the adjacent BNZ Buildings 1–4. It was a statement building, however, designed for an ambitious company by an outstanding architect, Frederick de Jersey Clere, then in partnership with his son Herbert.

   The building was the third on the same corner site to be erected for the Australian Mutual Provident (AMP) Society. Architectural quality kept pace with AMP's business success as a two-storey building (1877) was replaced with a masonry building (1897) of similar size, and then with the existing eight-storey building. Above a raised basement of New Zealand granite, and over a concrete-encased steel frame structure, the building is clad in warm-hued Sydney sandstone, probably hewed from the city's Pyrmont quarry; the building would look right at home on Macquarie Street, in Sydney's CBD. The AMP Building is a Chicago-style stretching of the palazzo model. It ascends from a double-height bottom (punctuated with a frieze and entablature) through a five-storey middle to a top composed of a cornice, attic floor and simple pediment. The windows get different Classical pediments at each floor, and at the seventh floor they are separated by bas-relief panels. Although the AMP has long departed the well-preserved building, its legacy remains. The chamfered corner elevation is still surmounted by the AMP's signature statue and motto — 'Amicus certus in re incerta' (A certain friend in uncertain times) — as is the marble-encased, barrel-vault main entry, which deserves a peek.

Huddart Parker Building

1 Post Office Square (2–6 Jervois Quay)

Crichton, McKay & Haughton, 1925

The tight grid of streets to the east of Lambton Quay emerges from the shadows at the small Post Office Square, named after the General Post Office (1912) which once occupied the adjacent block now claimed by the Intercontinental Hotel. The GPO, a four-storey, granite-clad Renaissance-style building designed by Government Architect John Campbell, was demolished in 1974, at the start of an era of civic vandalism in Wellington. A few decades later the Huddart Parker Building, directly overlooking Post Office Square, could have suffered the same fate but was saved and strengthened and retains its form as a tidy exemplar of the Chicago School. The building was constructed for the Huddart Parker shipping company, which was founded in Melbourne in 1876 and operated on trans-Tasman routes from the 1890s until its demise in the early 1960s. (In notable New Zealand maritime incidents, the Huddart Parker ship *Wimmera* was sunk by a German mine in 1918 off Cape Maria van Diemen, and in 1947 the company's trans-Tasman liner *Wanganella* ran aground at the entrance to Wellington Harbour.)

Crichton, McKay & Haughton designed the Huddart Parker Building with a rusticated two-storey base, four-storey 'shaft' and a seventh floor sandwiched between two cornices. The main entrance has a balustraded hood, and small balconies are sparingly and symmetrically deployed on the second and seventh floors of the building's three elevations (north, east and corner). The building's entrance looks out to a former tram shelter (Wellington City Engineer, 1912) that has housed a landmark newsagent since 1945. For decades the business was owned by Clarrie Gibbons, a rugby administrator who must have found his shop's location very convenient: the Huddart Parker Building was for many years the 'Kremlin', the headquarters of the New Zealand Rugby Union in the period when the tight-lipped organisation seemed to be running the country's foreign policy.

Government Life Insurance Building (Former)

50–64 Customhouse Quay and Brandon and Panama Streets

**John Thomas Mair, Government Architect,
Public Works Department, 1938**
Historic Place Category 2

From the perspective of the present, big buildings from early last century got finished fast. Hardly had the plans been unveiled, it seems, than dignitaries were gathering to celebrate the completion of construction. The Government Life Building, however, was an exception to the pattern of expedition. Soon after the 1931 Napier earthquake the government, conscious of the vulnerability of Wellington's unreinforced masonry structures, demolished the three-storey building of the Government Life Insurance company on reclaimed Customhouse Quay. The Government Architect's office under John Thomas Mair designed a new eight-storey building at the same location, though on a larger site. But construction didn't get under way until 1935, when 70 steel caissons filled with 7000 tons of concrete were driven down to bedrock. Local newspapers checked in on progress for the next several years — the reportage sadly included accounts of worker injuries and even death — before the building was occupied in stages from late 1938. Accidents were not unexpected on a project of such scale, but may have been related to the novel structural system employed — steel framing adapted, the media reported, from 'the form of construction used by the foremost Japanese authorities of earthquake-resisting building design'.

The massive building, which faces three streets, is an impressive meeting of the inter-war Stripped Classical and Moderne styles. A granite base is continued, Chicago-style, by a shaft vertically enhanced by slender piers and pretend pilasters, and topped by a simple cornice and pediment. Ornament is present, but hardly exuberant: two fluted columns framing the recessed portico; Art Deco panels between upper-floor windows; and the nicely done four-level oriels on the south and north corners.

20 Customhouse Quay

Studio Pacific Architecture, 2019

Once a decade, roughly, for the past half-century, Wellington has generated a significantly large building. At the start of the 1980s it was the BNZ Centre (see pages 168–69); at the beginning of the 1990s it was the Majestic Centre (see pages 160–61) and at the end of the 1990s, Te Papa (see pages 38–41); in the early 2010s, Telecom Central (see pages 166–67); and just before the start of the 2020s, the building at 20 Customhouse Quay. Te Papa spreads itself along the harbour while the BNZ Centre, Majestic Centre and Telecom Central all soar above Willis Street. 20 Customhouse Quay, though, is dominant in both directions, being 14 storeys high and a city block wide, and courtesy of its shiny glazed and faceted façade it bosses the west side of Wellington Harbour.

There's something about the building's height-to-width ratio and the proportions of its triangular facets — the surface of the eastern façade curves 2.4 metres and tilts 0.28 metres — that suggests thwarted ambition. The building looks like it's just getting going before it comes to a stop. (If it was in the City of London, for example, it would be three times as tall.) However, if it had achieved its implied potential the building would have made Lilliputians of all its neighbours. More to the point, the building's size must be the result of a complex financial algorithm factoring in construction costs, market capacity and, crucially, seismic resistance. A diagrid structure, alluded to in the façade and evident in the V-shaped supports on the ground-level plinth, has been allied to base isolators to produce a building that can safely shift 0.65 metres laterally in a 'one-in-2500-year' earthquake. The state-of-the-seismic-art building was generated by a close collaboration between Studio Pacific Architecture and engineering company Dunning Thornton.

Brandon's Building (Former)

150–152 Featherston Street

Francis Drummond Stewart, 1930

The term 'International Style', which was given to the mature Modernism that dominated the developed world's architecture in the decades after the Second World War, implies a global hegemony that was unprecedented. But the design styles of metropoles had long been exported to remote possessions and dependencies. Look at the Baroque architecture of New Spain, for example, or the Gothic Revival and English Baroque buildings which manifested Britain's imperial presence. Often, even the intramural style wars of wealthy and powerful countries had a ripple effect a long way from home.

The late-1920s design of Brandon's Building is an interesting exhibition of the contemporary differences, architecturally speaking, between New York and Chicago. (It also illustrates the gravitational cultural pull of the United States, despite New Zealand's attachment to Britain.) Brandon's Building probably constitutes a narrow win on points to New York, specifically to the Skyscraper style that flourished in the city in the 1920s and 1930s, famously in buildings such as the Chrysler and Empire State Buildings (both 1932) but also in earlier towers such as the Barclay-Vesey and Fred F. French Buildings (both 1927). Chicago School buildings terminated in a pronounced capital that performed the function of a Classical entablature, but the New York Art Deco skyscraper reached for the sky, its tapering form both a response to local setback prescriptions and an expression of boundless aspiration.

Eight-storey Brandon's Building follows the Chicago regime of base–shaft–capital but Art Deco vertical mouldings are attached to the top floor like roosting birds of prey and the building has its own little setback — a rooftop box that was originally a caretaker's apartment — and a fine display of brass spandrel panels. The building was designed for Brandon's, a Wellington legal dynasty, by Francis Drummond Stewart, then the house architect of the building's contractor, the Fletcher Construction Company.

Dominion Farmers' Institute Building

110–118 Featherston Street and Ballance Street

Collins & Harman, 1919
Historic Place Category 2

In 1915, you wouldn't have thought New Zealand's farmers were short of political influence. The prime minister, William Massey, was himself a farmer, and his conservative Reform Party was the stronger partner in the war-time coalition government. The country's economy was almost totally dependent on agricultural production, and militant labour unions had been defeated in the 1913 Great Strike. Still, in politics it never pays to be taken for granted and, prompted by Arthur Leigh Hunt (1876–1968), a leader in the farmers' co-operative movement, rural groups established the Dominion Farmers' Institute to promote their interests. Some of the Institute's formation capital of £75,000 — a large sum to raise during a world war — was immediately dedicated to building a Parliament-proximate Wellington headquarters that would be both office and social hub. (The brief called for three floors of hotel rooms for visiting farmers.) Hunt wanted 'a proven structure of distinctive architecture'. The Gothic Revival style was still synonymous with distinction, and few New Zealand architects were as practised in the genre as the Christchurch firm directed by John James Collins (1855–1933) and Richard Dacre Harman (1859–1927).

Collins & Harman duly designed a six-storey building — eight, including the mansard levels — that at the time of its completion in 1918 was allegedly one of the largest reinforced concrete structures in the southern hemisphere. In contemporary photographs, the building has the perpendicular grace of a Gothic cathedral. Slender piers ended in pinnacles, and the windows on several floors were framed with thin mullions and pointed arches. On the apex corner, a tower with oriel windows and a large upper-level Gothic arch was topped by a turret. Much of the ornamentation was removed after earthquakes in 1942, and major refurbishments in the 1960s and 1980s flattened the building's depth and fattened its proportions.

Wellesley Club (Former)

2–8 Maginnity Street

Gray Young, Morton & Young, 1927
Historic Place Category 1

Middle- and upper-class males in Victorian Britain were clubbable types. Emigration did not lessen their appetite for bourgeois bonding in gendered seclusion, and in colonial New Zealand they kept each other's company in controlled membership organisations ranging from volunteer militia units and yacht clubs to professional associations and learned societies. But for homosocial hanging-out, nothing could beat the gentlemen's club. Replicating this London institution was evidently a priority in early Wellington. Three gentlemen's clubs were set up in the two years following the arrival of the New Zealand Company's first ship in 1840. One, the Wellington Club — named, like the city, after the Duke of Wellington — was so enduringly well-subscribed that in 1891 it spawned an offshoot, the Junior Wellington Club. This was soon retitled the Wellesley Club (Arthur Wellesley being the family name of the Duke of Wellington). The Wellesley Club's first premises were damaged by fire and a 1907 replacement building designed by William Chatfield proved to be too small by the 1920s. Club member William Gray Young designed a new building on the corner of Maginnity and Ballance Streets. Gray Young liked the Georgian style (see pages 230–31) and saw its use as particularly appropriate for the Wellesley Club as it recalled the era of the 'Iron Duke'.

The Wellesley Club is a well-proportioned five-storey building made of reinforced concrete clad with English-bond brick. Balconies with metal balustrades separate the rusticated ground floor, with its round-arch openings, and upper levels with square-headed windows; the attic storey's dormer windows poke above the building's parapet. Oak and rimu panelling lined games rooms, lounges, library and dining room. Bedrooms were located on the upper floors. The building, which is to receive base-isolation strengthening, today operates as a boutique hotel; the Wellesley Club folded in 2014.

Missions to Seamen Building
(Former)

7 Stout Street and Whitmore Street

Crichton & McKay, 1903
Historic Place Category 1

The Missions to Seamen was founded in 1850s England as an Anglican organisation ministering to seafarers, and subsequently spread around the world. It still operates, as the Mission to Seafarers, in 200 ports in 50 countries. Reverend James Moore (1854–1932) arrived in Wellington in 1898 to set up a branch at the busy port, and got on energetically with his mission to care for seamen in distress, provide wholesome alternatives to traditional sailor shore pursuits and, of course, evangelise for Jesus. After several years of itinerant operation, Moore received a windfall. Mary Ann Williams (c1839–1920), widow of Wellington ship owner Captain William 'Bully' Williams (1832–1890), donated £7000 to the mission. This was a huge sum; in fact, said *The New Zealand Times*, Mrs Williams's gift was 'the finest instance of philanthropic spirit that has been manifested by any citizen of Wellington, perhaps the whole country'. Moore promptly bought a plot of harbour-adjacent reclaimed land and commissioned a building from the firm of Crichton & McKay (see pages 104–05).

The architects designed a double-storey building with a hall on the ground floor and a church upstairs, both spaces large enough to accommodate 400 people. There was also an office, tearoom, library and caretaker's flat. The design of the plastered brick and concrete Missions to Seamen building has been described as Edwardian Free Style; that is, it is an eclectic mix of neo-Gothic pointiness, evident in the pitched roof and gables on the north and west façades, and neo-Classical curviness, demonstrated in the arches above the entrance and the upper-level windows. The mission sold its building to the government in the 1970s; a decade later, a public campaign thwarted the Labour government's intention to demolish the building which, in 1994, was converted into 10 apartments (architect unknown).

Hotel Waterloo

1 Bunny Street and Waterloo Quay

Atkins & Mitchell, 1937
Historic Place Category 2

Not far from the club (see pages 218–19) which bore the
Duke of Wellington's family name, a hotel was built with a title
memorialising the field marshal's most famous victory. One
day, when 'Aotearoa' and 'Te Whanganui-a-Tara' have naturally
succeeded — or at least been conjoined with — 'New Zealand' and
'Wellington', respectively, the settler habit of treating 'their' new
land as a toponymic terra nullius may just seem to be something
the country had to grow out of. The remembrance of imperial
heroes, British battles and English towns may come to be perceived
as an expression of insecurity as much as ignorance, and the
place name props might then be redundant. In the meantime, the
anachronisms abound. Hotel Waterloo opened its doors 122 years
after Napoleon's fate was decided at the eponymous Belgian village.
The building had been commissioned by New Zealand Breweries,
hotel owner as well as beer maker, to coincide with the completion
of the adjacent Wellington Railway Station (see overleaf).

Cyril Hawthorn Mitchell and his brother Allan, still trading
under the practice's old name of Atkins & Mitchell, designed what
may have been Wellington's first podium-and-tower building. The
hotel's tower elements — each four storeys high, plus a recessed
top floor — were arranged so that all 102 rooms would benefit from
the corner site's ample natural light. The restrained Art Deco styling
includes decorative bands along the top of the podium and the two
upper levels. When new, the hotel was hailed by the press as 'the
last word in modernity and comfort'. Public areas had maple walls
and chrome fittings; bedrooms were centrally heated and equipped
with 'latest type telephones'. The heyday of the hotel was during
the 1940s and 1950s; for 30 years, it has waged a long rearguard
action as a backpackers' hostel.

Wellington Railway Station

2 Bunny Street, Waterloo Quay and Featherston Street

Gray Young, Morton & Young, 1937
Historic Place Category 1

Trains have played a bigger part in the history of Wellington than in that of any other New Zealand city, and the main railway station has been a landmark civic feature for more than 80 years. Considering the importance of rail, the building was a long time coming. The first railway station in Wellington occupied timber structures erected at the Thorndon end of the harbour in 1874; the station burned down four years later. The government and a private company — later nationalised — then built two small stations serving suburban and regional lines. The need for a proper station increased with the completion in 1908 of the Main Trunk Line between Wellington and Auckland. Before the First World War the government tied the construction of a new station and its associated marshalling yards to a proposed harbour reclamation in the Thorndon area. That reclamation, which filled in 28 hectares of the harbour, began in 1924 and was not completed until 1932.

In the meantime, in 1929, the government commissioned Gray Young, Morton & Young to design Wellington Railway Station, settling on a 4 per cent design fee for a project estimated to cost £470,000. There was no design competition for the new building; presumably the other contender for the commission was Gummer & Ford, the firm that designed Auckland Railway Station, which opened in 1930, and was shortly to design the National Art Gallery and Dominion Museum (see pages 136–37). It is interesting that the Government Architect's office, designer of much of New Zealand's infrastructure, was not entrusted with railway work.

Gray Young, Morton & Young designed a six-storey building in the neo-Classical genre that was the default style for inter-war governments of every political persuasion. The design influence, in a zeitgeisty rather than explicit way, was probably McKim, Mead & White's Pennsylvania Station (1910) in New York. (The Beaux-Arts masterpiece was controversially demolished in the mid-1960s.) Like the much grander Penn Station, Gray Young's Wellington station combined a Classically ordered exterior with a generous and ornate interior. The building, as big railway stations once were, was a temple to travel. A forecourt serves as a mini-agora in front of the main façade, which centres on a colonnade of eight Doric columns, 13 metres high, surmounted by a clock and simple pediment.

Through the entrance is one of Wellington's finest interior spaces — the station booking hall, with its terrazzo floor inlaid with a compass design, granite and marble walls decorated in mottled dados, and vaulted ceiling. The concourse, with its concrete arches and glazed roof, was designed to have the ambience of a 'vast sunroom'. Station amenities included a hairdressing salon with showers and plunge baths, dining room, book shop and top-floor nursery staffed by a kindergarten teacher and Plunket nurse.

Construction occurred in the context of the Depression. This was both a challenge for the government (in terms of finding the money to pay for the building) and an opportunity (to provide jobs). The station was a huge project: the building covered 0.6 hectares and was 105 metres long on its western, Featherston Street side. It required more than 1500 reinforced concrete piles to support 2000 tons of steel framing, 25,000 tons of Hutt River aggregate and 1.75 million cladding bricks, many slotted to accommodate steel reinforcing rods. Construction, under the supervision of 26-year-old Fletcher project manager Joe Craig, did not start until 1934, by which time Gray Young, Morton & Young had been forced to amend the design. The Featherston Street wing and an extension to the Waterloo Quay wing were added in the late 1930s.

At the station's opening on 19 September 1937, the attention of invited guests was, noted *The Dominion*, diverted by 'the overhead drone of a new aeroplane nearing the end of a test flight from Auckland to Wellington in the record time of two hours five minutes'. The newspaper was right to recognise a harbinger of the transport future, but the fate of Wellington Railway Station was also in the hands of politicians. In the late twentieth century, the railways were restructured, downsized and generally degraded. Wellington Railway Station still functions as the terminus of a busy suburban network, but much of the building is now occupied by Victoria University, having been redeveloped in the early 2000s by Athfield Architects.

ROUTE 5:
WEST SIDE

CIRCA 3 KILOMETRES

This route begins with the little cluster of star-gazing and weather-watching buildings at the top of Wellington's Botanic Garden, which itself offers a network of pedestrian paths and panoramic views of the city. (A cable car ride from Lambton Quay is the way to reach the start of the route, unless you're feeling fit and adventurous.) Then it's downhill, past the university and along The Terrace, with its apartments and corporate offices, to the government part of town, with its mix of neo-Classical, Gothic Revival and Brutalist buildings. The route ends at one of Wellington's most significant heritage sites, Old St Paul's Church, but has an addendum — another religious building, Futuna Chapel. The deconsecrated chapel is a bit out of the way — it's 5 kilometres from Old St Paul's and the nearby Railway Station/ Bus Terminus — and infrequently open, but if the stars align, the Modernist icon is worth a visit.

To Futu
Chape

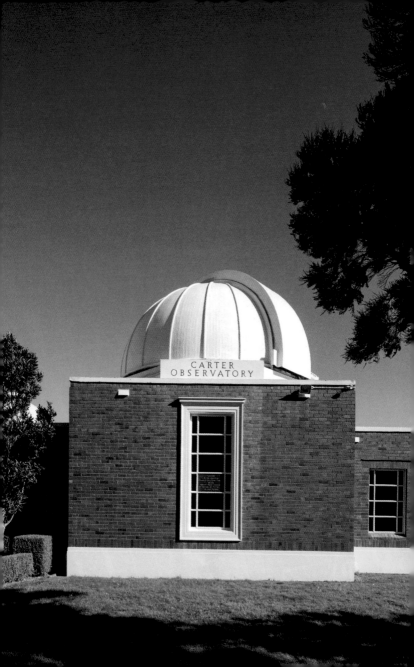

Carter Observatory

40 Salamanca Road

Gray Young, Morton & Young, 1941
Historic Place Category 2

In 1868, on a site in the Bolton Street cemetery, the government built an observatory to determine accurate time through 'observing' the transit of stars. The Time Service observatory was demolished to allow for the burial of Prime Minister Richard Seddon (1845–1906) and replaced at the top of the Botanic Garden with the Dominion (Hector) Observatory (see overleaf). In the late 1930s it was decided to build a new observatory, with greater research capacity. Funding came from the 1896 bequest of successful contractor Charles Rooking Carter — surely one of the few instances in New Zealand history where compound interest has outpaced the rising costs of construction. Once the Carter Observatory opened in 1941, with new telescopes and more staff, the adjacent Hector Observatory, which already recorded earthquake activity, focused exclusively on its seismological function. (The amateur astronomers of the Wellington Philosophical Society were also observing the heavens from this patch of the Botanic Garden, from the simple, timber-clad and still extant Thomas King Observatory, designed by Government Architect John Campbell in 1912.)

The Carter Observatory was designed in the office of the prolific practice of Gray Young, Morton & Young, and probably should be attributed to William Gray Young (see pages 82–83, 200–01, 218–19, 224–27). Gray Young's partiality for the Georgian style is given typically symmetrical expression in the flat-roofed podium, constructed of brick-faced reinforced concrete, that supports the original two spheres of the observatory's domes. The building's design is rather sepulchral; it's all about the astronomy. The Carter Observatory became the national observatory in 1977, but increasing light pollution hindered its operation and it lost its status in 2010. It is now, having been indifferently added to and altered over the years, a visitor and education centre.

Dominion Observatory
(Hector Observatory)

Botanic Garden, 34 Salamanca Road

John Campbell, Architect, Public Works Department, 1907
Historic Place Category 1

Nestled in the lee of a ridge above the CBD, the 25-hectare Wellington Botanic Garden offers respite from the southerlies, the city and the twenty-first century. The garden is almost as old as the city itself. Before European settlement, the site the garden now occupies provided food for Te Āti Awa from Pipitea pā. In 1844, land was set aside for a botanic garden, which was officially established by an Act of Parliament in 1869. The Botanic Garden was a very Victorian creation, combining a Romantic attachment to wild nature, a belief in the public health benefits of urban parkland and a commitment to useful scientific research. The garden was used as a 'Central Depot for botanical and acclimatising purposes'. (The hazards of the exotic animal acclimatisation programme were demonstrated in the attacks on children by escaped monkeys.) In the 1890s, the city council took over the Botanic Garden, and as its use shifted to public recreation it received a gentler Edwardian overlay, including a tearoom, band rotunda and playground.

In its first two decades, the Botanic Garden was managed by James Hector (1834–1907), whose dominance of New Zealand science — he was director of the New Zealand Institute, Geological Survey, Meteorological Department, Colonial Laboratory, Colonial Museum and Colonial Observatory — gave rise to the term 'Hectorian centralism'. Hector was memorialised in the name originally given to the 1907 observatory designed by John Campbell (1857–1942), then architect in the Public Works Department, and soon to be Government Architect. Built above the remains of a gun battery dating from the 'Russian Scare' of 1885, the observatory is an Edwardian Baroque masonry pavilion with a transit room (see previous pages) and octagonal tower. A plaster render was applied to façade elements, including the base, cornice, parapet, horizontal banding, and corner and window quoins.

Wellington Meteorological Office

30 Salamanca Road

William Alington, Architectural Division, Ministry of Works, 1968

William (Bill) Alington belongs to a talented group of Wellington architects who were students at Auckland University's School of Architecture in the late 1940s and early 1950s, and whose later careers intersected for several decades. Like his peers James Beard, William Toomath and Derek Wilson, Alington spent formative years overseas at a time when Modernism was a meaningful movement. Alington was a cadet with the Ministry of Works (MoW) before going to university, and he returned to the MoW before taking up a Fulbright Scholarship. He worked in London for Robert Matthew, Johnson-Marshall & Partners, the practice designing New Zealand House (1963); made the pilgrimage to Modernist architectural sites such as Le Corbusier's Chapel of Notre-Dame du Haut (1955) at Ronchamp; and studied for a master's degree at the University of Illinois, just a couple of hours from Chicago and the Lake Shore Drive Apartments (1951), one of the great buildings by his favourite architect, Ludwig Mies van der Rohe (1886–1969).

Back in Wellington and working for the MoW under Government Architect Fergus Sheppard (1908–1997), Alington applied his learning to the design of the Meteorological Office, located at the top of the Botanic Garden, adjacent to the Dominion and Carter observatories (see previous pages). The four-storey concrete building has a Miesian boldness, even if it lost much of its Miesian rhythm with the removal of its bands of pre-cast concrete shade fins. The architectural drama is supplied by the projecting top floor, which houses weather forecasting equipment; viewed from below, this cantilever seems to float above the surrounding trees. Over time, the Meteorological Office has settled comfortably into its site, perhaps confounding doubts about its appropriateness. Brutalist architecture and botanic gardens can, it turns out, get on very well together.

Chevening

90 Salamanca Road

Llewellyn Edwin Williams, 1929
Historic Place Category 2

Even with years lost to the Depression, Wellington experienced an apartment boom between the wars. From a standing start, more than 30 substantial apartment buildings went up in the 1920s and 1930s. Reinforced concrete construction and the market response to demographic realities — not everyone needed or wanted to live in a standalone suburban house — combined to produce a more urbane and sophisticated city. Chevening is a symbol of this emerging diversity. The building was commissioned by Emma Margaret Rainforth (1872–1936), a University of Otago mathematics graduate who pursued a career as a teacher, firstly in Auckland, at a Methodist high school, and from 1912 to 1927 at Wellington Girls' College. Rainforth was well-travelled — she spent some years in Europe and also went to India — and was active in women's, educational and church organisations. She 'gained the respect and devotion of all among whom she lived and worked', her obituary recorded, and she possessed a 'strength that made her triumphant against weakness and disappointment'.

Chevening — the title probably refers to the Kentish village and seventeenth-century country house of the same name — was a retirement project for Rainforth, providing her with an income as well as a home. She occupied the top floor of the four-storey building, which has one apartment per floor. (The ground-floor apartment is smaller, to accommodate garaging.) The design by Llewellyn Edwin Williams, a graceful blend of Stripped Classical and Art Deco, is distinguished by the two canted bays that project, one further than the other, on either side of a kind of extruded Classical portico. Decorative brickwork and painted panels fill in the spaces between the façade's slimming pilasters. In 2019 the building, which had been restored in 2011 by Studio Pacific Architecture (project supervision: Lianne Cox), was gifted to Heritage New Zealand Pouhere Taonga.

Hunter Building

Victoria University of Wellington, Kelburn Parade

Penty & Blake, 1906, 1909; Swan & Lawrence, 1922, 1923
Historic Place Category 1

Wellington was comparatively late in getting a university. The city lagged behind Dunedin (1869), beneficiary of the gold rushes, Christchurch (1873), servant of a wealthy pastoral hinterland, and Auckland (1883), already the largest city. But in 1897, the sixtieth year of Queen Victoria's reign, Parliament established Victoria College of Wellington, and once a bare hillside in the new suburb of Kelburn had been selected as the institution's site the government ran a design competition. It was won by the short-lived (1903–1909) but prolific (more than 100 commissions) firm of Penty & Blake. Yorkshireman Francis Penty designed army barracks and railway buildings before coming to New Zealand in 1887. In Wellington, he was a city councillor, founder member of the Institute of Architects, enthusiastic lawn bowler and generous charitable donor. Edward McCallum Blake (1865–1929) was born to missionary parents in Bangalore. He grew up in Dunedin, where he was 'schooled' as an architect and worked in Canterbury and Victoria before practising in Wellington, ambitiously. 'There isn't a lot of E.M.,' noted a 1909 newspaper profile, 'but all there is of him hustles.'

In designing Victoria College, Penty & Blake used the perpendicular Collegiate Gothic style, redolent of Oxbridge tradition. Only the Arts and Science components of the design were realised when the building opened in 1906. The Arts block, in red brick and cream Ōamaru stone, puts its best Gothic face forward with its gables, mullions, buttresses, pinnacles and battlements. This block was extended in 1909, and north and south wings, both designed by Swan & Lawrence, were added in 1922 and 1923. For many years, before trees grew and neighbours jostled, the Hunter Building was locked in a Gothic gaze with St Gerard's Church and Monastery (see pages 50–51) on the other side of the city. Even now, the Hunter Building remains the architectural symbol of Victoria University.

Jellicoe Towers

189–191 The Terrace

Allan Wild, Williams Construction, 1968

Jellicoe Towers — a plural name for a single building — would seem to be a prime example of architecture tempting fate. Sited at the top of an escarpment in a city straddling a major fault line and subject to howling gales, the tall, skinny apartment building looks thrillingly vulnerable. However, it has endured for more than half a century, a testimony to the talent of architect Allan Wild (1927–2019) and engineer Lyall Holmes (1920–1970). Wild's confidence in the durability of his design was tested when he went to the top of the building, then nearing completion, during the storm — at the time, the worst ever recorded in New Zealand — that sank the *Wahine* in April 1968; the experience assured him that Jellicoe Towers was Wellington-proof.

The 18-storey apartment building, which is constructed around a central lift core, has one three-bedroom flat per floor; floor-to-ceiling windows in the living areas offer expansive views of the city. At each level, the floor slabs project from the exterior walls, providing horizontal articulation to a slim form designed to minimise visual obstruction. The slender grace, and generous amenity, of Jellicoe Towers is perhaps surprising, given the project's provenance. Wild designed the building when he was employed by Arthur Williams (1928–2001), a hard-nosed property developer and horse-breeder. Before working for Williams, Wild had been an associate with Porter & Martin (see pages 54–55), partnered with Anthony Treadwell (1922–2003), and served as architect-in-charge at Wellington City Council. When a student at the University of Auckland, he participated in one of the key moments in New Zealand Modernism, the foundation of the Architectural Group, later to become Group Architects. Not long after the construction of Jellicoe Towers, Wild returned to the University of Auckland as Dean of the Faculty of Architecture, a position he held from 1969 to 1993.

Herbert Gardens

186 The Terrace

Biggs, Power & Clark, 1965

The inter-war years had seen a sprouting of apartment buildings
— admittedly modest in scale — around inner Wellington, but the
immediate post-war decades were given over to suburbia and its
sprawl. There were, though, a few locations that bucked the trend.
One was Oriental Parade; another was the upper end of The Terrace.
Named, very literally, for its positioning on a terrace running along
the ridge above Lambton Quay, The Terrace is one of Wellington's
most notable streets and from early on it was a fashionable address.
Over time, it acquired a commercial character at its north end, while
many of the substantial timber houses further up the rise were
gradually converted to flats accommodating Victoria University of
Wellington students.

　　One of these big houses was Fern Glen, an 1880s mansion
occupying an acre of land at 186 The Terrace. In the 1920s Dr
William Herbert, founder of Wellington's first private hospital,
moved into Fern Glen, which had been owned by the family of his
wife, Florence. The Herberts were philanthropists, and Florence's
commitment to charity survived her husband's death in 1933. In
March 1934, for example, *The Evening Post* noted her 'beautiful
garden' was the scene of a fundraising event for the Wellington
Free Kindergarten featuring 'a well-stocked cake and produce stall',
mannequin parade and 'demonstration of physical culture'. After
Florence Herbert died in 1961, her house was demolished — much
of the garden was later requisitioned for motorway construction
— and replaced by Herbert Gardens, a 13-storey, concrete and
glass Modernist tower with 52 apartments. The T-shaped building,
designed by the short-lived practice led by architect Denis Gordon
Biggs (1926–2009) and engineers Cedric Arthur Power (1926–
2021) and Jack Enoch Clark (1912–2001), is more substantial than
neighbouring Jellicoe Towers (see previous pages), but shares with
it a crisp horizontal delineation provided by projecting floor plates.

Franconia

136 The Terrace

Edmund Anscombe & Associates, 1938
Historic Place Category 2

Edmund Anscombe believed in progress and the ability of design, planning, technological innovation and industrial production to solve socio-economic problems, such as a shortage of decent urban housing. In this, although he lived far from the epicentres of Modernism, Anscombe was attuned to the spirit of an age that generated the Bauhaus school in Weimar, Germany, and the proselytising International Congresses of Modern Architects, co-founded by Le Corbusier in 1928. Anscombe put his principles into practice by commercialising a concrete construction system (see pages 66–67), producing the architectural components of the 1940 New Zealand Centennial Exhibition in Wellington, and advocating for multi-unit social housing schemes. He designed one such complex himself in 1936, and took his proposal for 18 five-storey apartment buildings in the working-class suburb of Newtown to the city council, which was interested, and the new Labour government, which was dismissive. 'Frankly, I do not like flats,' said cabinet minister and future prime minister Peter Fraser. 'I think they are alien and foreign to the country.'

What Anscombe did get built in the late 1930s were several apartment buildings for the middle-class rental market, two of them at Oriental Bay (see pages 56–57, 66–67) and one, Franconia, on The Terrace. Squeezed between the street and a rear cliff, Franconia is a six-storey reinforced concrete building which had two flats on each of its first and second floors and one on each of the upper levels; ground-floor garages were soon converted to shops. Anscombe gave Franconia his favoured Streamline Moderne treatment. Classical pilasters are used as motif on the street façade and the architect's familiar trope of a multi-storey oriel window makes its appearance on the north elevation. A tower of curved windows turns the north-west corner of the building. All the flats were converted into offices in the 1960s and 1970s.

Shell House (Former)

96 The Terrace

Stephenson & Turner, 1960

The construction of Shell House at the end of the 1950s was a key event in the transformation of the lower half of The Terrace from a residential row to a commercial canyon. It was one of the first glass curtain-wall towers in the city, and, because this façade system was used on all sides except the west elevation overlooking the motorway, the building is perhaps an even more overt expression of its type than the earlier Massey House (see pages 182–83). The building was designed in the Wellington office of Stephenson & Turner, then an Australian-owned firm but today a New Zealand-only concern.

Commissioned as the national headquarters for the eponymous petroleum company, Shell House was a break-out project for Stephenson & Turner, which in this country had hitherto specialised in hospital architecture. Accordingly, the practice pulled out all the stops in designing a state-of-the-art office tower. The building has a lightweight steel frame erected around a reinforced concrete structural core housing lifts and services and providing seismic and wind resistance. It is clad in alternating bands of green and black tinted glass framed with anodised aluminium. (Concrete aggregate panels are used on the west façade.) A commitment to innovation extended from construction techniques, especially the off-site fabrication of elements such as floors, framing and internal fixtures, to occupier experience — Shell House was probably New Zealand's first fully air-conditioned building. The podium had an exhibition area and 100-seat theatre (since removed). The design influence is clear: Lever House (1952), the Manhattan tower designed by Gordon Bunshaft (1909–1990) and Natalie de Blois (1921–2013) of Skidmore, Owings & Merrill. But Lever House has 21 floors to express its elegance, Shell House has 11; in its case, less is not more.

Braemar Flats (Former)

32 The Terrace

Crichton, McKay & Haughton, 1924/25
Historic Place Category 2

For more than 80 years following its foundation in 1840, Wellington was faced with twin existential threats. In a timber town, fire was a constant threat but masonry construction was not an especially reassuring alternative when every decade brought a significant earthquake. It's easy to see why reinforced concrete was enthusiastically embraced as a building material in the early twentieth century. As well as its application in larger-scale commercial architecture, the technology enabled denser habitation of the residential areas around the city centre. Reinforced concrete, and a growing service economy, ushered Wellington into modernity in the years after the First World War. This was the Golden Age of the medium-rise apartment building in the city, with four- and five-storey flats going up on fashionable streets such as Oriental Parade and The Terrace.

As testament to the appetite for apartment living, Braemar Flats was a speculative project, sited next to the new St Andrew's Church (see overleaf) in what was still a neighbourhood of stand-alone houses. Designed by the partnership founded in 1901 by William Crichton and James Hector McKay and joined in 1923 by Vivien Haughton, Braemar is a five-storey reinforced concrete building — a penthouse with a caretaker's flat was added in 1927 — with a tōtara and rimu interior. Braemar had three flats per floor; medical doctors had offices on the ground floor, and for several decades the upper-floor flats were occupied by middle-class professionals and reasonably affluent widows. (Braemar is now commercially tenanted.) The building, somewhat Art Deco in style and painted Sienna brown, is notable for its four-level, bow-fronted oriels — reminiscent of Clere & Williams's 1923 Inverleith apartments (see pages 70–71) — on the east and north façades, and its projecting cornice.

St Andrew's

28–30 The Terrace

Clere & Williams, 1923
Historic Place Category 1

By the early 1920s Fredrick de Jersey Clere had been practising architecture in New Zealand for more than 40 years. His latest business partner was Llewellyn Edwin Williams, successor in that role to William Baldwin Busby (1891–1917), who had been killed while serving in a British regiment in Mesopotamia. Clere and Williams had hardly completed their work on St Mary of the Angels (see pages 154–55), a replacement for a burnt church, when St Andrew's Presbyterian church on The Terrace became another of the city's fire casualties. The timber building had been constructed in 1878, to the design of Danish immigrant architect Christian Julius Toxward (1831–1891). Not surprisingly, church leaders decided the new St Andrew's would be built of concrete.

Clere & Williams produced a rectangular design in the tradition of the relatively restrained version of the Baroque style that held sway in England in the later seventeenth and early eighteenth centuries, the period dominated by Sir Christopher Wren (1632–1723). It is a work by one of Wren's protégés, James Gibbs (1682–1754) — St Martin-in-the-Fields, London (1726) — that suggests itself as an ancestral relative of St Andrew's. Like Gibbs's grander church, St Andrew's features a tower that progresses from a square base to an octagonal summit, a portico with a triangular pediment, and Classical columns. (St Andrew's has the full set — Doric, Ionic and Corinthian.) It should be noted that Toxward's earlier church also had a pedimented and columned tower. In terms of its fittings and fixtures, St Andrew's, which was designed to accommodate 600 worshippers, is plain, as Presbyterians prefer, but the interior is distinguished by a fine coved ceiling and round chancel arch. When built, the church was a commanding presence in its part of town; now it is dwarfed, but not diminished, by indifferent office towers.

Turnbull House

25–27 Bowen Street

William Turnbull, 1916
Historic Place Category 1

Colonial New Zealand had three outstanding collecting maniacs (book division) whose personal libraries were to form the basis of important public collections. Governor and premier George Grey (1812–1898) left thousands of books and manuscripts to Auckland Library; Dunedin doctor Thomas Hocken (1836–1919) assembled a book collection now held by the University of Otago; and Wellington business scion Alexander Turnbull (1868–1918) donated the biggest library of all — 55,000 items — to the state, which keeps it as part of the National Library. Turnbull was a metropolitan aesthete who was perhaps never quite at home in settler society. His father was a Scottish merchant who came to Wellington in 1857 and returned to England, wealthily, in 1875, keeping his New Zealand business. Born in Wellington, Alexander Turnbull was educated in London, where he joined his father's company; he twice visited New Zealand in the 1880s before arriving more definitively in 1892. He worked in the family business, golfed, owned yachts, and belonged to learned societies — the Royal Geographical Society, Linnean Society, Polynesian Society — and the Wellington Club. But his passion was collecting books, his main interests being New Zealand and the Pacific, Victorian intellectual John Ruskin and seventeenth-century poet John Milton.

Around the time of the outbreak of the First World War Turnbull, who had no family of his own, commissioned a house — a kind of duplex, half for himself and his servants, half for his books — from the unrelated William Turnbull, who, perhaps out of filial piety, had kept the practice name Thomas Turnbull & Son. The three-storey brick and concrete house, with its prominent two-storey bay windows, is stylistically eclectic; heritage researcher Natalie Marshall discerns Scottish Baronial, Queen Anne and medieval influences. In the 1970s the government wanted to demolish the building; a popular protest saved it, but it still awaits seismic strengthening.

Parliament Executive Wing
('The Beehive')

Parliament Grounds, Bowen Street and Lambton Quay

Basil Spence and Ministry of Works, 1982
Historic Place Category 1

It's an enduring legend of New Zealand architecture: the parliamentary building drawn on a napkin and justified by reference to the logo on a box of matches. By the early 1960s governments and members of Parliament had had plenty of time to regret the decision to build only the first half of John Campbell's Edwardian Baroque Parliament House (see overleaf). More office space was needed. The options were to demolish the existing building and start again, or complete the original design, or commission a contemporary addition. The Ministry of Works (MoW) and Government Architect Fergus Sheppard supported the latter course — like good Modernists, Sheppard and his colleagues believed that to repeat the past was to betray the present.

Fortuitously — or not — the celebrated British architect Sir Basil Spence (1907–1976) had been invited to lecture in Wellington in 1964 and the government decided to ask him what it should do. (Even at the time, this recourse was derided as the colonial cringe in action.) Spence's Brutalist Coventry Cathedral (1962) had recently opened, and his reputation was at its zenith. (It declined later, along with the reputation of Brutalism.) As architects are inclined to do when asked for an opinion, Spence went further and produced some sketches — drawn on a pad, not a napkin — and showed them to parliamentarians. Spence's 'germ of an idea' for an Executive Wing housing cabinet ministers was for a circular building, a 'peg in the ground' stabilising a sloping site, its form an echo of the curve of the Bowen Street and Lambton Quay junction. He dubbed the design the 'beehive', and apparently reinforced the metaphor by showing a box of Beehive-brand matches to the prime minister. Taking 18 years, the MoW — Spence-less, as time went on — delivered a 10-storey conical building with floors of decreasing diameter rising above a rectangular podium and concluding in a copper crown.

Parliament House

Parliament Grounds, 1 Molesworth Street

John Campbell, Government Architect, Public Works Department, 1922
Historic Place Category 1

In Wellington's Alexander Turnbull Library there's a watercolour based on the winning scheme in the 1911 design competition for Parliament House. It paints an impressive picture: a long, colonnaded, symmetrical building sited, Parthenon-like, on a rise, and composed, Louvre-like, of a central portico under a large dome flanked by pavilions with cupolas. Less than half of the design was built. A shame, really, but also an outcome so typical as to be axiomatic: if parts of an ambitious design are deferred, the odds are they'll never be built. At least, not as originally conceived. In architecture, as in life, moments pass, things move on.

Parliament House, which contains the Legislative Chamber, replaced timber Parliament buildings destroyed by fire in 1907. The design competition for a masonry building attracted 33 entries, two of them, to the consternation of local architects in private practice, submitted by the Government Architect, John Campbell. One of Campbell's entries, produced with colleague Claude Paton (1881–1953), was awarded first prize; the other, a collaboration with Charles Lawrence (c1873–1933), also a colleague, took fourth prize. The final design apparently drew from both of Campbell's entries. Like most competition entrants, Campbell defaulted to the English Baroque house style of the British Empire. As built, Parliament House consists of two pavilions, the larger serving as the entry portico, linked by a loggia with Ionic columns. Clad in granite from Coromandel and marble from Kairuru, near Motueka, the building is an extravaganza of Baroque gallimaufry: rusticated stonework; pediments, quoins, keystones and festoons. Construction started under a Liberal government and stalled, after the war, under the successor Reform administration. In the 1990s, the building was seismically strengthened and internally reconfigured by Warren and Mahoney.

General Assembly Library
(Parliamentary)

Parliament Grounds, 1 Molesworth Street

**Thomas Turnbull; John Campbell, Public Works
Department, 1901**
Historic Place Category 1

The General Assembly Library is the Gothic member of a family
that also includes the Baroque Parliament House and the Brutalist
'Beehive'. It is the most picturesque of the three buildings, even
though it was disowned by its original designer. The library for the
General Assembly, as New Zealand's Parliament was styled at its
inception in the 1850s, was established in 1865 and for several
decades occupied half a dozen rooms heated by open fires. In 1897
Thomas Turnbull was commissioned by Premier Richard Seddon
to design a dedicated General Assembly library. Turnbull had
previously designed a brick addition (1883) to the timber General
Assembly building (1873), a work by the Colonial Architect William
Clayton. That building was neo-Gothic, and Turnbull matched
its form but, again, not its material. (It was by then accepted in
Wellington that wooden construction was not a particularly
prudent choice for a large structure, especially one housing
thousands of books.) Instead, Turnbull designed a building of
plaster-rendered, load-bearing bricks, made by prisoners at Mount
Cook Goal, on concrete foundations.

The building is a picturesque composition of gables, hipped roofs,
pointed arches, pinnacles, finials and rose windows with a suggestion
of Venetian tracery. As designed, the General Assembly Library had
three above-ground storeys; as built, it has two. The building's Gothic
verticality was compromised when Seddon was forced by political
and media critics of his 'monstrous' extravagance to reduce its height.
Turnbull was not amused and withdrew from the project, which
was completed by John Campbell, then lead architect in the Public
Works Department. The building proved its worth when it survived
the 1907 fire that destroyed the adjacent Parliament buildings. It was
strengthened and renovated in the 1990s by Warren and Mahoney.

Wellington Cathedral of St Paul
(New St Paul's)

2 Hill Street and Molesworth Street

Cecil Wood; King & Dawson; Miles Warren, 1964–2001

The intersection where Hill, Aitken and Molesworth Streets meet is a tough architectural site. On opposite corners, two bruisers make their stand, one of them, the National Library (see overleaf) secular; the Cathedral of St Paul, religious. The cathedral, which succeeded Old St Paul's (see pages 266–69) as the Anglican 'mother church' in Wellington, is a textbook illustration of the challenges of delivering, in modern times, a type of building that historically was constructed very slowly. It's not just that the longer completion takes, the sooner a design will date; it's also a matter of the changes that happen along the way. A comparison with St Mary of the Angels (see pages 154–55) highlights St Paul's situation. The inspiration for St Mary's (1922) was, apparently, a medieval Belgian cathedral, but Clere & Williams got away with their atavism because the church was built quite quickly, it was not that prominent, and Modernism had not yet arrived in New Zealand.

Cecil Wood, the leading Christchurch inter-war architect, was denied those advantages after being commissioned to design St Paul's in 1937. Wood's design for the concrete cathedral was, as his former pupil Miles Warren wrote, 'idiosyncratic'. Naturally, Wood was trying hard. Warren, who was invited to finish St Paul's in the 1990s, pointed to the cathedral's Spanish Mission, Nordic National Romantic and even Byzantine influences. There are Art Deco elements, Gothic gargoyles and a suggestion of Moorishness. Wood died before the foundation stone was laid in 1954, and King & Dawson continued, and altered, the project from the 1960s to the 1980s. Warren then redesigned the narthex, adding a touch of Luxor to what Modernist critics had called the cathedral's 'jigsaw of trappings'. It is an awkward building, but also interesting, and seen to best advantage from the National Library café on Molesworth Street.

National Library of New Zealand

70 Molesworth Street and Aitken Street

Architectural Division, Ministry of Works, 1987

Wellington has some tough examples of concrete Modernism, and the National Library is one of the toughest of them all. The building was provocatively hard at the time of its completion in 1987 and although alterations have made its interior more welcoming it retains its uncompromising public demeanour. There's something admirable about that, to architects, at least. The building is another example of the power of resolutely modern architecture to alienate professional appreciation from popular opinion. The Ministry of Works (MoW), the government's design-and-build agency from the 1940s to the late 1980s and the producer of the National Library, was not much concerned with public sentiment. The real threat to its discretion came from its ministerial masters, who turned the money taps on and off according to economic circumstance or political whim. This dependence had inevitable implications for government building work.

The National Library project started in 1970 and took 17 years to finish. Over that time, the thinking around a 'national library' evolved; an institution set up to safeguard important materials was, increasingly, expected to promote access to them. The National Library was reimagining itself even as it moved into a building designed as a cultural Fort Knox. John Boyes, an architect in the Architectural Division of the MoW, began sketch plans for the library four years before foundation work started in 1974; a tender for the rest of the building was issued in 1978; and then the building was redesigned to remove steelwork, and therefore the Boilermakers Union (see pages 168–69), from the project. The obvious reference is another concrete inverted ziggurat, Boston City Hall (1968), also a polarising piece of Brutalism, designed by Kallmann, McKinnell & Knowles under the spell of Le Corbusier's monastery of Sainte Marie de La Tourette (1960) near Lyon.

Freyberg Building

20 Aitken Street

Architectural Division, Ministry of Works, 1979

The late 1970s was the high-water mark for the government as designer and builder for the nation. By then, the Ministry of Works (MoW) had had several decades of growth under both centre-right (National) and centre-left (Labour) governments. MoW engineers and architects had produced a huge number of infrastructure projects, ranging from power stations and motorways to hospitals, universities and courts. Under the Government Architect, the MoW's Architectural Division was well staffed and, recalls Duncan Joiner, the section's head in its final, late-1980s iteration, 'frantically busy'. Looking back, Joiner sees the MoW as an 'architectural supernova', burning bright before its collapse following the election in 1984 of the privatising Labour government.

One of the legacies of the MoW and its architects is a group of buildings designed as civil service offices in the area around Parliament. (The distribution of the buildings preserved views of and from Parliament House.) Planning for the Government Centre precinct started before the Second World War and implementation proceeded from the 1950s to the early 1980s. This was a Modernist project with Modernist architecture. Nationalist and economic imperatives governed decisions about design and construction; local industry and the country's balance of payments were supported by specifying New Zealand materials. Reinforced concrete was the universal structural medium, and the Vogel Building (1966) even had a timber curtain wall and boiler fuelled with (New Zealand) coal. The Freyberg Building was one of the last of the Government Centre buildings, and it and the National Library (see previous pages) are alone in keeping their original façades. MoW architect Peter Sheppard supervised the design of a building tall enough, at 15 storeys, to achieve a proper proportionality, and with a façade given generous depth by 3-foot floor projections. The building remains faithfully Brutalist; it needs a deep clean but hopefully will escape the indignity of a recladding.

Old St Paul's

34 Mulgrave Street

Frederick Thatcher, 1866
Historic Place Category 1

In mid-nineteenth-century England, Gothic was the architectural language of the godly. Gothic Revivalism was not then a style, but a movement — styles always start out as something meaningful — and it came with its own vanguard party, the Ecclesiological Society, founded at Cambridge University in 1839. The Ecclesiologists sought to renew Anglicanism by reviving the rituals of the medieval church and the architecture in which they were performed. They wanted, literally, to reconstruct the Middle Ages, taking pious inspiration from the soaring, made-you-look-up architecture of the great Gothic cathedrals. The well-connected members of the Ecclesiological Society were powerful architectural influencers. Overcoming accusations of 'Popishness', they made their Gothic point, you could say, in the arches and spires of scores of new or reconfigured churches. It should be noted, too, that the Gothic Revival in England was also buttressed by secular figures, most prominently John Ruskin, author of the great pro-Gothic polemic *The Stones of Venice* (1853).

The revival of Gothic architecture was well under way in England as settlement started in New Zealand. It is therefore not surprising that adherents of ecclesiology turned up in the colony, and not just in Anglican-founded Christchurch, the destination of New Zealand's outstanding Gothic Revival architect Benjamin Mountfort. In 1843 Frederick Thatcher (1814–1890), a Gothic Revival architect from London, arrived in New Plymouth, taking up a portion of the land 'acquired' by the New Zealand Company. With his new wife, Caroline, Thatcher soon left for Auckland, where he benefited from the patronage of Governor George Grey in gaining various official appointments. He then trained as a Church of England minister, entering the orbit of George Augustus Selwyn (1809–1878), the first Anglican bishop of New Zealand, and a patron of the Ecclesiological Society. In the 1840s and early 1850s, Thatcher pursued his religious career while also working as an architect, designing numerous small wooden 'Selwyn' churches around Auckland. After some years back in England, he returned to New Zealand in 1861, serving for several years as vicar of St Paul's in Wellington, and, again, as Selwyn's architect. (He resettled in England in 1868.)

In 1862 Thatcher designed a new church for St Paul's parish on a lot that had been bought by Selwyn and augmented by Grey's grant of some land set aside as Māori reserve. Thatcher did what he usually did, and did well: he designed a church that ideally, for an ecclesiologist, would have been made of stone in the timber materials locally at hand. As it turned out, the substitution was serendipitous. Thatcher designed a rectangular building, aligned east–west, with the entry at the west, under a spire. A baptistry, nave and aisles led to the altar at the liturgically correct east end of the church. The straightforward plan, it transpired after the church was consecrated in 1866, was a bit too simple: the building's form made it vulnerable to Wellington's winds. In the first of several interventions by leading Wellington architects of their day, Christian Julius Toxward designed two tethering transepts, the north added in 1868, the south completed in 1874. Frederick de Jersey Clere extended the baptistry and designed some other alterations in the 1880s, and William Gray Young added a women's vestry in 1944.

It is the wooden realm of its interior that makes St Paul's one of New Zealand's most important buildings. Kauri, rimu and tōtara may not have the implacable timelessness of stone, but Gothically deployed as piers and vaults the timbers convey the ecclesiological message of calm transcendence in a rich, warm tone. St Paul's was effectively Wellington's Anglican cathedral from 1866 until enough of New St Paul's (see pages 260–61) became usable in 1964. A strong heritage campaign was mounted to save Old St Paul's when the building was deconsecrated. The Ministry of Works subsequently restored the church, with architect Peter Sheppard, though a practising Brutalist (see pages 264–65), demonstrating considerable sensitivity as he supervised the preservation of St Paul's Gothic Revival integrity. Old St Paul's is now managed as a historic site by Heritage New Zealand Pouhere Taonga.

Futuna Chapel

67 Futuna Close, off Friend Street, Karori

John Scott, 1961
Historic Place Category 1

Icon is a word overused in architecture to the point of exhaustion but if there's one building in New Zealand to which the term can be meaningfully applied it's Futuna Chapel. Architects might not agree on everything — or much at all — but there is consensus that Futuna Chapel is the country's most intriguing and singular Modern-era building. Searching for an analogue commentators have turned to Le Corbusier's Chapel of Notre-Dame du Haut (1955) in Ronchamp, north-eastern France. Like that definitely iconic building, Futuna Chapel is sui generis. It's impossible to separate the building from the story of its creation and its architectural creator.

John Scott (Ngāti Raukawa, Te Arawa, Ngāti Kahungunu; 1924–1992) was 34 when he was asked to design the chapel for a retreat centre in suburban Karori run by the Society of Mary (Marist) order of the Catholic Church. It seems extraordinary that an organisation known primarily as an operator of schools that combined traditional pedagogy and a commitment to rugby union should have turned to a young Modernist architect, and have ended up with such a radical building. But architecture has always been an exception to the cultural conservatism of the Catholic Church and its agencies — witness Ronchamp, for example. Plus, Scott had a reassuring pedigree. He had been head prefect, and captain of the First Fifteen, at St John's College, a Marist high school in Hastings. Not long out of Auckland University's School of Architecture, he returned to St John's to design a chapel (1956), and shortly afterwards was commissioned to design Our Lady of Lourdes Church (1960) in nearby Havelock North.

The Marists had commissioned one of their own, Brother Albert Kelly, formerly an architect (see pages 108–09), to design Futuna Chapel, named for the Pacific island where Marist missionary priest Pierre Chanel was martyred in 1841. But the conservative proposal of 70-year-old Kelly disappointed his more imaginative superiors and they approached Scott. The making of the chapel was quite a trip: a charismatic and creatively autonomous architect designed an original building which was constructed by a group of largely unskilled workers — Marist brothers — whose labour compensated for their order's lack of capital. Contemporary photographs portray construction scenes that are almost medieval — labourers with hand tools clambering up roofs pitched as steeply as the spires on a Gothic cathedral. Scott was often around; according to one account, 'additional details were often drawn up on site on a piece of wood using a carpenter's pencil carried around on an ear'.

Futuna Chapel's materials were simple and economical — timber framing; concrete walls with a stucco render forgiving of imperfections; an asbestos-tiled roof — but its form is complex. The square plan is bisected by an east–west diagonal axis leading from the double-entry porch to the altar. On each side small altars extend beyond the walls. In the centre of the building a large post carries the roof peak, and its struts support the roof planes. The roof is where the chapel gets complicated, as the quadrants into which the building is divided are resolved as steeply vertical triangles. The result, internally, is a soaring volume, atmospherically illuminated courtesy of Perspex 'stained glass' windows designed, as were the Stations of the Cross and figure of crucified Christ, by artist Jim Allen.

Futuna Chapel is a building that has to be experienced to be comprehended, if not defined. It is always referenced in discussions about the emergence of an architecture indigenous to or expressive of Aotearoa New Zealand. How 'Māori' is the building? Citing especially the key pou tokomanawa, or central post, architectural historian Russell Walden hailed the chapel as a fusion of Māori and European architecture. Architect and writer David Mitchell didn't go that far, but still saw evidence of Māori/European crossover in the chapel's design, while historian Bill McKay is more inclined to view the building as 'assimilationist' rather than bicultural. John Scott didn't leave explicit explications to guide Futuna's later interpreters: he wasn't the type to climb into any convenient box. Futuna Chapel was endangered when the Marist order sold their retreat site to a developer in 2000; however, a trust rallied to save and restore the building. The deconsecrated chapel hosts public architectural events several times a year.

ARCHITECTURAL STYLES AND INFLUENCES

Art Deco: An architectural and design style popular in the 1920s and 1930s that took its name from the 1925 Exposition Internationale des Arts Décoratifs et Industriels Modernes in Paris. In architecture, Art Deco was a highly stylised version of Modernism that blended sleek forms, contemporary materials and bold colours to self-consciously glamorous effect.

Baroque: In continental Europe, Baroque was the exuberant style of the sixteenth and seventeenth centuries' Counter-Reformation — an architecture of exaggerated effect, with lavish façades and theatrical interiors. In England, as seen in the architecture of Christopher Wren (1632–1723), the style was tempered with Classical elements. At the turn of the twentieth century in Britain and its colonies, the style was revived and became the architectural expression of late British imperialism, expressed in hefty and august buildings much adorned with ornamental elements. In this incarnation, the style goes under various names — Baroque Revival, English Baroque, Edwardian Baroque.

Bauhaus: The influential and free-thinking school established by architect Walter Gropius in Germany's inter-war Weimar period that championed functional and rational design and the use of mass-produced industrial materials. After the Nazis shut the institution down in 1933, Bauhaus Modernist precepts were spread throughout Europe and the United States by the school's teachers and students, underpinning the International Style which became dominant in the years following the Second World War.

Beaux-Arts: The rich, Classically influenced architectural style promulgated by the École des Beaux-Arts in Paris from the mid-nineteenth century through the first few decades of the twentieth century. Around the world, a Beaux-Arts architectural education was based on a near-slavish devotion to gaining fluency in the architectural language of Classical antiquity.

Brutalism: The term coined in Britain in the early 1950s — derived from 'béton brut' (raw concrete) — to characterise the Modernist architecture of Le Corbusier and applied to monolithic poured-concrete buildings with clearly expressed or emphasised structural elements. The style, also known as 'New Brutalism', endured in New Zealand until the early 1980s.

Chicago School or Style: Relates to the late nineteenth- and early twentieth-century steel-framed, high-rise architecture that evolved in Chicago, and the architects, such as Louis Sullivan (1856–1924) and Daniel Burnham (1846–1912), who produced it. Many Chicago tall buildings expressed the three parts of a Classical column: base of lower floors, shaft of middle storeys, and capital of topmost levels. The post-war non-historicist skyscraper architecture of, most notably, Ludwig Mies van der Rohe (see page 278) and the firm of Skidmore, Owings & Merrill is sometimes said to constitute a Second Chicago School.

Classicism and Classical Revivalism: The Greek and Roman architecture of Classical antiquity formed the basis for Renaissance architecture and was revived in the nineteenth and early twentieth centuries in both relatively austere (e.g., Stripped Classical) and more grandiose (e.g., Second Empire) styles. Common characteristics of these revivals were a concern for symmetry and adoption of or at least allusion to the components of the Classical architectural orders (Doric, Ionic, Corinthian).

Collegiate Gothic: A sub-genre of Gothic Revival architecture popular in the late nineteenth and early twentieth centuries on school and university campuses.

Edwardian and Edwardian Free Style: The somewhat toned-down version of the High Victorian Baroque Revival style, but likewise inspired by French eighteenth-century architecture and the English seventeenth-century 'Wrenaissance'. A popular style for public buildings in the late British Empire, featuring cupolas and central towers, rusticated bases, pediments, columns, keystones and quoins. John Campbell's Parliament House is a prominent Wellington example of the style.

Edwin Lutyens: Originally an Arts and Crafts architect, Lutyens (1869–1944) became famous for the neo-Classical buildings and monuments that made him the leading British architect of his generation.

French Second Empire: A stylistic evolution during the reign of Napoleon III (1852–1870) of French Renaissance and Baroque architecture that produced a Classically influenced, symmetrical styling most effectively applied at scale to larger buildings. Columns and low domes were often deployed; a distinguishing characteristic is the mansard roof.

Georgian: Classically influenced architecture of symmetry, restraint and well-considered proportions, using masonry materials, that held sway in Britain in the Hanoverian era (1714–1837), and continued to be revived as a popular style in Anglophone societies into the first half of the twentieth century.

Gothic: An architectural style dominant in much of late medieval Europe. Gothic buildings, especially churches and cathedrals, had many pointy elements — gables, spires and lancet windows — and were shored up with buttresses that allowed vertical extension and countered the lateral thrust of vaulted roofs. The nineteenth-century revival of the Gothic style was associated with High Church Anglicanism, and was introduced to New Zealand by architects linked with the Gothic Revival ecclesiological movement in England. Gothic architecture was stone architecture, but Gothic churches in Wellington, and Auckland, were often built of wood.

The Group: A post-war cohort of architectural students at the University of Auckland who advocated for a 'New Zealand' realisation of Modernist architectural principles and subsequently founded a construction company to produce economic and place-appropriate timber houses.

High-tech: An architectural style that emerged in the late 1970s in which a building's structure, preferably made from modern industrial materials such as steel, aluminium and glass, and mechanical services are exposed. Flexible spaces and bright colours are other characteristics of the style.

International Style: A style of Modernist architecture developed and disseminated by Le Corbusier and Bauhaus alumni, including Walter Gropius and Ludwig Mies van der Rohe. The style emphasised functional performance and formal clarity and eschewed ornamentation; it was characterised by flat roofs and smooth surfaces, including large glazed areas often expressed as curtain walls, and constructed of modern, mass-produced materials. As its name suggests, the style became globally ubiquitous as the default for corporate office buildings.

Italianate and Italian Renaissance: Architecture of the fifteenth and sixteenth centuries that followed the rediscovery of the cultures of Classical antiquity. Revived in nineteenth-century Britain and then spread to the colonies, it was usually deployed on buildings of some substance. The picturesque Italianate style was characterised by the symmetrical disposition of such Classical elements as towers, cupolas, cornices and corbels.

La Tourette: In full, Sainte Marie de La Tourette — a priory near Lyon designed by Le Corbusier and completed in 1961. The architect referred to his final building, which is a Brutalist concrete structure raised on pilotis, or columns, as an 'Assyrian fortress'. Like the chapel of Notre-Dame du Haut, La Tourette is a destination for the serious architectural pilgrim.

Le Corbusier: Prime candidate for title of 'architect of the twentieth century', the Swiss-born French architect Charles-Édouard Jeanneret (1887–1965), known as Le Corbusier, was an enormously influential designer, theorist, writer and urban planner. He realised his own 'Five Points' or principles — pilotis (concrete columns); free (open) plan; free (separated) façade; horizontal window; and roof garden — in buildings that married Modernist functionalism and sculptural expressiveness.

Metabolism: The post-war Japanese architectural movement that posited, and produced, buildings composed of cell-like parts capable of replication and replacement in an organic process of renewal.

Ludwig Mies van der Rohe: German-born Ludwig Mies van der Rohe (1886–1969) was the architect of some of the greatest works of Modernist architecture, including the Barcelona Pavilion (1929); Lake Shore Drive Apartments (Chicago, 1951); Farnsworth House (Plano, Illinois, 1951); and the Seagram Building (New York, 1958). His architecture is famous for his masterful use of modern industrial materials to produce buildings of extraordinary purity and clarity of form.

Moderne: Also called Art Moderne or Streamline Moderne — the boundaries of the terms are rather blurred — Moderne was a comparatively restrained inter-war iteration of Art Deco, and cautious anticipation of the full-blown Modernism of the International Style. Moderne architecture was characterised by curved forms and horizontal lines — Art Deco played up vertical elements — and often by ship-like styling and nautical detailing.

Modernism: The most important architectural style or movement of the twentieth century. Modernism was characterised by a rejection of ornamentation, the belief that a building's form should follow from an analysis of its function, and a commitment to the rational use of contemporary industrial materials and building technologies. In New Zealand, after a slow start, Modernism was the architectural orthodoxy from the Second World War to the end of the 1970s.

Palazzo: A style of late nineteenth- and early twentieth-century building based on the town houses (palazzi) of Italian Renaissance patrician families. The building type — solid and symmetrical, and more austere than buildings in 'Italian Villa' mode — was particularly popular with late Victorian-London gentlemen's clubs.

Post-modernism: An eclectic and individualistic style often incorporating historicist playfulness and whimsy which emerged in the late 1960s and 1970s as Modernism ran out of steam as a democratic movement and declined into predictable conformism and global ubiquity.

Romanesque: A pre-Gothic style of medieval architecture featuring semi-circular arches for windows and doors, vaults to support the roof, and massive piers and walls.

Ronchamp: The name of a village in north-eastern France near the Swiss border given as shorthand title to the local hilltop Chapel of Notre-Dame du Haut (1955) designed for a Catholic society by Le Corbusier. A concrete building with an expressive form composed of thick, curved walls pierced by small windows, many of stained glass, and a dramatic upturned roof.

Spanish Mission: An early twentieth-century architectural style derived from late eighteenth- and early nineteenth-century Spanish colonial buildings in California. The style, characterised by stucco walls with a curvilinear gable shape or low parapets at the roof line, enjoyed some popularity in New Zealand in the inter-war period.

Villa Savoye: The influential house at Poissy on the outskirts of Paris designed by Le Corbusier and completed in 1931. The functionally and formally purist building, which was an expression of the architect's Five Points of Architecture, was the first French Modernist building to be designated as an historic monument.

Vitruvius: More properly Marcus Vitruvius Pollio (c80–70–c15 BCE), a Roman architect and engineer and author of the 10-book architectural treatise *De architectura*. Famous for his formulation that all buildings should possess three attributes: firmitas (strength); utilitas (utility); and venustas (beauty). His discussion of the ideal proportions of the human (male) body prompted Leonardo da Vinci's famous drawing of the Vitruvian Man.

GLOSSARY OF ARCHITECTURAL TERMS

Acroteria: Plinths for statues or ornaments on top of a pediment; also refers to the statues themselves. Singular form: acroterion.

Aedicula: In Classical Roman architecture a small shrine housing a statue; in Beaux-Arts design, a door or window framed with columns or pilasters and crowned with a pediment.

Architrave: The lowest of the three main parts of a Classical entablature: the beam spanning the columns and resting on the capitals.

Ātea: On a marae, the open area in front of the wharenui (meeting house) where formal welcomes and debates are staged.

Baptistry: Area within a church, or often a separate structure, for conducting baptisms.

Bargeboard: Protective board, often ornamentally carved, used on the edge of gables where the roof extends over the wall.

Base isolation: Seismic-resistant technology, much used in Wellington, in which flexible bearings and layers of rubber and/or lead absorb ground movement to protect a building's structure.

Bracket: Element on a building's façade giving visual, or actual, support to overhanging features such as cornices and balconies.

Brise soleil: A fixed (and on more recent buildings, moveable) horizontal or vertical sunshade façade element.

Buttress: Mass projecting from or built against a wall to counter the lateral thrust of roof vaults and arches.

Caisson: A watertight chamber driven down to a firm foundation level and filled with concrete; often used on reclaimed sites, such as those around Wellington Harbour.

Capital: The head or crowning member of a column, pilaster or pier; the Classical orders each have their distinctive capitals.

Chancel: The space around the altar at the east end of a church, traditionally reserved for the clergy and choir.

Chevron: 'V' shaped motif that, vertically arranged in series, was a favourite ornamental component of the Art Deco style.

Classical orders: Styles of columns, capitals and entablature derived from the architecture of ancient Greece and Rome. The Doric style is the plainest, the Ionic is more ornamental, and the Corinthian is the most ornamental of all. The Composite style is a Roman combination of the Greek Ionic and Corinthian orders.

Clerestory: An upper level or row of windows that admits light into a building.

Cloister: A space, usually quadrangular, enclosed by an arcade or covered walkway.

Column: Vertical, circular load-bearing or ornamental member consisting of base, shaft and capital.

Console: Ornamental curved bracket, often moulded or sculpted, applied to a wall of a building.

Corbel: Projecting block, usually of stone, supporting a horizontal structural element.

Corinthian: The most ornate of the architectural orders or styles of ancient Greece, which features a slender, fluted column on a raised base, with a capital of stylised acanthus leaves. Named for the city-state of Corinth.

Cupola: Small dome crowning a roof or turret.

Diagrid: Framework of diagonally intersecting beams.

Cornice: In Classical architecture, a shelf or moulding projecting from the top of a building; the uppermost part of the entablature.

Curtain wall: A non-load-bearing wall attached to a building's structure; in Modernist architecture, often a glass wall applied to a steel frame.

Dentil: Small square block used in series as a moulding, usually under the cornice of buildings in the Classical tradition.

Doric: Simplest of the Classical orders; columns in this style have a relatively short shaft, no base and undecorated capital. Named for the Doric-speaking peoples of ancient Greece.

Dormer window: A window, housed in its own structure, that projects from a sloping roof; so called because it often serves an attic-level bedroom.

English-bond: Bricks laid in alternate courses of headers (short sides facing outwards) and stretchers (long sides facing outwards).

Entablature: Upper part of a Classical building, supported by columns, and comprising the architrave (the lintel above the columns), frieze (the decorative band above the architrave), and cornice (the horizontal moulding at the top of a building).

Festoon: Carved or moulded façade ornament in the form of a ribboned garland of fruit and flowers.

Finial: An ornament, commonly foliated or leaf-shaped (often like a fleur-de-lis), on top of a spire, gable or pinnacle.

Frieze: Central section of an entablature, between the architrave and cornice, often decorated with sculpture in low relief.

Gable: Triangular upper portion of a wall between the edges of intersecting roof pitches.

Hipped roof: Roof which slopes upwards, usually gently, from all four sides of a building, and thus has no gables.

Ionic: Classical order midway in its ornamentation between the Doric and Corinthian orders; fluted columns sit on simple bases and are topped with capitals with spiral volutes. The architectural order or mode originated in the Greek cities of Ionia in Asia Minor (present-day western Turkey).

Keystone: Central stone of an arch.

Lancet window: A slender, pointed arch window typical of early Gothic churches of the twelfth and thirteenth centuries.

Loggia: A gallery or arcaded structure open to one or more sides; can be a colonnaded porch attached to a building.

Maihi: On a wharenui, the diagonal bargeboards, signifying the building's arms, at the gable's front edge.

Mansard roof: A roof with a double slope, the lower being steeper and longer than the upper. Occurs often in eighteenth- and nineteenth-century French buildings; its advantage is that it economically provides a spacious attic storey.

Marae: A complex of buildings and spaces that includes an ātea (courtyard), wharenui (meeting house) and whare kai (eating house).

Mullion: Vertical element that divides a window into two or more sections.

Narthex: Porch or entry foyer in a church of a Basilica type; that is, rectangular in shape, with a nave and aisles terminating in an apse, or semi-circular vault.

Nave: The central part of a large church, usually stretching from the entrance to the transepts, and accommodating the congregation.

Oriel window: A type of bay window that protrudes from the main wall of a building, usually from an upper floor, supported by a corbel, or bracket.

Palazzo: An Italian Renaissance palace or grand residence built by wealthy families.

Parapet: Extension of a wall along the edge of the roof, originally designed for defensive purposes.

Pedestal: In Classical architecture, the base supporting a column or colonnade; more generally, the base for a superstructure.

Pediment: Classically derived low-pitched triangular gable surmounting a façade or doors and windows; may also be straight-edged or segmentally curved.

Pendant: An ornament suspended from a ceiling or vault.

Piano nobile: The main, or 'noble', floor of a house with 'public' or reception areas; usually the first floor.

Pier: A solid masonry support; can be free-standing, but more substantial than a column, or may be integrated with a wall.

Pilaster: A shallow or partial version of a rectangular column or pier projecting from a wall; usually conforms to one of the Classical orders.

Pilotis: Columns or pillars that support a building, thereby leaving the ground floor completely or partially open.

Pinnacle: Decorative apex, usually pyramidal or conical in shape, that terminates a spire or buttress.

Polychromatic: Variously coloured, to provide architectural interest, e.g., bands of differently coloured bricks on a façade.

Portico: Covered building entrance, usually a roof or arch, supported by columns.

Quatrefoil: Type of window tracery formed by a circular arrangement of four foils, or leaf shapes; quatrefoil windows were a feature of Venetian Gothic palaces.

Quoin: A dressed stone to mark a building corner or edge; a feature that was often adopted in nineteenth- and early twentieth-century New Zealand timber architecture.

Reredos: Decorated wall or screen behind a church altar.

Rondel: Small circular decorative device used in relief on a building façade.

Rusticated: A masonry — or, in New Zealand, even a timber — façade designed to give the appearance of quarried stones separated by recessed joints.

Spandrel: The triangular space on a façade between the sides of adjacent arches and the line across their tops. Can also refer to the area between the sill of a window and the head of the window below it, and on steel or reinforced concrete buildings may be a beam between columns or piers.

Swag: A type of festoon, often in the form of a cloth or garland of leaves draped between two supports.

Transept: Transverse arm of a cross-shaped church — one of the two areas that flank the nave, or main body of the building.

Tympanum: Triangular space between the mouldings of a pediment; also the space between the lintel over a door and the arch above.

Vestry: Small building or structure attached to a church where clerical vestments and religious vessels are stored.

Volute: Small scroll on an Ionic capital.

Wharenui: Communal or meeting house that is the focus of a marae.

SOURCES AND FURTHER READING

Compared to other New Zealand cities, Wellington is well served with sources of information and publications about its architecture. A very helpful city council website has descriptions of significant Wellington heritage buildings and profiles of the practices and architects who designed them (www.wellingtoncityheritage.org.nz). A good overview of the city's development is provided in the council's *Thematic Heritage Study of Wellington* (2013), available online at www.wellington.govt.nz/-/media/arts-and-culture/heritage/files/thematic-heritage-study.pdf. The council also publishes a series of pamphlets — in printed and downloadable versions — dedicated to various 'heritage trails'. Google's ubiquity might attract criticism, but its Google Maps and Street View tools are very helpful to anyone wanting to locate buildings on their streets and in their contexts.

Heritage New Zealand Pouhere Taonga, the government heritage agency that designates 'historic places', lists them online, often with extensive descriptive text (www.heritage.org.nz/the-list). The official heritage list is dominated by pre-Second World War buildings, but Modern-era architecture is increasingly represented on it. Te Kāhui Whaihanga New Zealand Institute of Architects offers a snapshot of recent Wellington architecture in the awards section of its website (www.nzia.co.nz).

Te Ara — The Encyclopedia of New Zealand (https://teara.govt.nz/en) has short biographies of many of the prominent architects who have practised in Wellington, as noted below. Papers Past (https://paperspast.natlib.govt.nz/) is the National Library's online archive of New Zealand newspapers, which at present covers the period from 1839 to 1961. For this book, Wellington newspapers *The Dominion*, *The Evening Post* and *The Free Lance* were particularly useful. (Architecture was more fully reported in New Zealand newspapers at the turn of the twentieth century than it is at the start of the twenty-first.)

One book deserves special mention: *Raupo to Deco*, a history — cited more fully below — of the first century of Wellington's post-European settlement architecture and architects by Geoff Mew and Adrian Humphris. In their book, the authors profile more than 100 architects active in the city from 1840 to 1940, and provide short notes on scores more. An invaluable resource, produced by indefatigable labour.

The following publications were helpful in the writing of this book, and are recommended to anyone in search of further reading about its contents:

AGM Publishing. *Architecture New Zealand: The Designing of Te Papa* (Special Issue, 1998).

Balasoglou, John, ed. *Stephenson & Turner*. Auckland: Balasoglou Books, 2006.

Barrie, Andrew. *Block Guides Map 3: A Guide to Wellington Architecture*. Auckland: Block/New Zealand Institute of Architects Auckland Branch, 2015.

Bevin, Nick and Gregory O'Brien, eds. *Futuna: Life of a Building*. Wellington: Victoria University Press with Futuna Charitable Trust, 2016.

Gatley, Julia. *Athfield Architects*. Auckland: Auckland University Press, 2012.

——, ed. *Long Live the Modern: New Zealand's New Architecture 1904–1984*. Auckland: Auckland University Press, 2008.

—— and Paul Walker. *Vertical Living: The Architectural Centre and the Remaking of Wellington*. Auckland: Auckland University Press, 2014.

Gordon, Alexander Latch. 'Another Elderly Lady to be Knocked Down: Heritage discourse and the protest to save the Missions to Seamen building, 1986'. Master's thesis, Victoria University of Wellington, 2018.

Helms, Ruth M. 'The Architecture of Cecil Wood'. PhD thesis, University of Canterbury, 1996.

Johns, Peter. 'Shifting Sands at Oriental Bay'. www.butterpaper.com. Posted 9 November 2019.

Joiner, Duncan. 'The Government Architect's Office, 1940–1992'. *Tāpoto — The Brief* 2 (2019).

Kernohan, David. *Wellington's New Buildings*. Wellington: Victoria University Press, 1989.

—— *Wellington's Old Buildings*. Wellington: Victoria University Press, 1994.

McCarthy, Christine. 'Anscombe's Plans for Highrise Living'. *AHA: Architectural History Aotearoa* 3 (2006).

—— 'High Modern'. *Architecture New Zealand* 2 (2006).

Mew, Geoff and Adrian Humphris. *Architects at the Apex: The Top 50 in New Zealand, 1840–1890*. Martinborough: Ngaio Press, 2020.

—— *Raupo to Deco: Wellington Styles and Architects 1840–1940*. Wellington: Steele Roberts Aotearoa, 2014.

Richardson, Peter. 'Building the Dominion: Government Architecture in New Zealand, 1840–1922'. PhD thesis, University of Canterbury, 1997.

—— 'The Government Architect's Office, 1869–1940'. *Tāpoto — The Brief* 2 (2019).

Sarnitz, August and Eva B. Ottillinger. *Ernst Plischke: The Complete Works*. Munich: Prestel, 2004.

Shaw, Peter. *A History of New Zealand Architecture*. 3rd ed. Auckland: Hodder Moa Beckett, 2003.

Skinner, Robin. 'Hanky-panky at Parliament'. *Architecture New Zealand* 2 (2005).

Stratford, Stephen, ed. *Four Architects 1950–1980: William Alington, James Beard, William Toomath, Derek Wilson*. Auckland: New Zealand Architectural Publications Trust, 2010.

Te Ara — The Encyclopedia of New Zealand. Biographies of: Edmund Anscombe (written by Greg Bowron); John Campbell (Peter Richardson); William Clayton (Anna Crighton); Frederick de Jersey Clere (Susan Maclean); William Ferguson (F. Nigel Stace); Reginald Ford (Peter Lowe); William Henry Gummer (Ian Lochhead); J. T. Mair (Peter Shaw); Ernst Plischke (Linda Tyler); John Scott (Russell Walden); Frederick Thatcher (Margaret Alington); Thomas Turnbull (Chris Cochran); Gordon Wilson (Julia Gatley); Cecil Wood (Ruth M. Helms); William Gray Young (Michael Fowler).

Walker, Charles, ed. *Exquisite Apart: 100 Years of Architecture in New Zealand*. Auckland: Balasoglou Books/New Zealand Institute of Architects, 2005.

Walsh, John. 'Nobody's Soldier: Gerald Melling in Profile'. *Houses NZ* 6 (2007).

—— *Stuart Gardyne: New Zealand Institute of Architects Gold Medal 2015*. Auckland: New Zealand Institute of Architects, 2015.

—— *Roger Walker: New Zealand Institute of Architects Gold Medal 2017*. Auckland: New Zealand Institute of Architects, 2017.

Warren, Miles. *Miles Warren: An Autobiography*. Christchurch: Canterbury University Press, 2008.

ACKNOWLEDGEMENTS

It has been a pleasure, after producing guides to the architecture of Auckland and Christchurch, to once more work with photographer Patrick Reynolds on this guide to Wellington's architecture.

We both thank publisher Nicola Legat for her commitment to architectural publishing, and her Massey University Press colleagues Anna Bowbyes and Emily Goldthorpe for their exemplary project management and editing. Thanks also to photo editor and post-production maestro Sjoerd Langeveld and to designer Imogen Greenfield for their skilful contributions. The Warren Trust and Resene lent generous support to the publication of this book.

At several sites, building owners or managers facilitated interior photography. Thanks to the Futuna Trust (Futuna Chapel), Heritage New Zealand Pouhere Taonga (Old St Paul's), Manatū Taonga Ministry for Culture and Heritage (Hall of Memories), and Te Herenga Waka–Victoria University of Wellington Faculty of Law (Old Government Building).

Over the years, conversations with Wellington architects have helped me to better understand the city and its architecture. I'd like to acknowledge in particular Gerald Blunt, Duncan Joiner, David Kernohan, Stuart Niven, Roger Walker, and the late Ian Athfield and Gerald Melling.

I'd like to acknowledge and thank the other peas in my Wellington pod, my cherished siblings Catherine, Frances and Michael. And finally, I couldn't have written this book without the support and encouragement of Catherine Hammond and Xavier Walsh. My thanks go to them, especially.

— John Walsh

INDEX

Architects

Practices

Engineers, builders, artists and makers

Buildings

First published in 2022 by Massey University Press
Reprinted 2022
Massey University Press
Private Bag 102904, North Shore Mail Centre
Auckland 0745, New Zealand

www.masseypress.ac.nz

A catalogue record for this book is available from the
National Library of New Zealand

Printed and bound in Singapore by Markono Print Media Pte Ltd

ISBN: 978-1-99-115110-0

The publisher is grateful for the support of
The Warren Trust and Resene

THE WARREN TRUST

the paint the professionals use